JOHN
The Word Became Flesh

*Jesus did many other miraculous signs in the presence
of His disciples, which are not recorded in this book.
But these are written that you may believe that Jesus
is the Christ, the Son of God, and that by believing
you may have life in His name.*

John 20:30–31

Prepared from Materials Provided
by Richard O. Reinisch

Compiled and Edited by Debb Andrus

CONCORDIA   PUBLISHING   HOUSE   ·   SAINT   LOUIS

Contents

Lesson 1

In the Beginning (John 1)

Theme Verse

"The Word became flesh and made His dwelling among us. We have seen His glory, the glory of the One and Only, who came from the Father, full of grace and truth" **(John 1:14).**

Goal

In this session we will look at what John says about Jesus as the Word of God who brings light and life, about the witness of John the Baptizer to Jesus, and about the witnessing of Andrew and Philip.

What's Going On Here

In Christian art the authors of the gospels are often represented by the four living creatures that John, the writer of the Revelation, saw standing around the throne of heaven **(Revelation 4:6–8).** Traditionally, it is held that the lion stands for Matthew, who presented Jesus as the Lion of Judah, the Messiah promised to the people of Israel. The ox stands for Luke, because Luke pictured Jesus as the sacrifice for all humanity and the servant of all. The man stands for Mark, who, more than any of the other gospel writers, drew attention to the full humanity of Jesus. The eagle stands for John, because the eagle soars toward heaven and because of all creatures it alone can look into the sun without being blinded. John's gospel carries us into the heights of God's eternal intention and fastens our gaze on the dazzling glory of God as it is revealed in Jesus Christ. John's purpose is clear. He intends to reveal the nature of God Himself as revealed in the promised Messiah, Jesus the Christ.

What we are studying is no impartial, objective history of some past event. This is a gospel, that is, Good News from God, Good News about the incarnation, life, death, and resurrection of Jesus Christ. John believed that Good News with his whole being. It changed his life. It gave him *life*, real *life*. He wanted everyone to share that *life*. And so as an old man, close to death, he put his experience and his understanding of God's Good News in writing. His purpose was to ignite and to strengthen faith, as he himself tells us: "Jesus did many other miraculous signs in the presence of His disciples, which are not recorded in this book. But these are written *that you may believe that Jesus is the Christ, the Son of God, and that by believing you may have life in His name*" (**John 20:30–31;** emphasis added).

Searching the Scriptures

The Prolog (John 1:1–18)

Read **John 1:1–18.** The gospels of Matthew, Mark, and Luke are called the synoptic gospels. The word *synoptic* means "affording, presenting, or taking the same or a common view." These gospels are called "synoptic" because they recount the life, death, and resurrection of our Lord in basically the same way. There is a common core of material, a basic outline of events that can be found in all three. John's gospel is different. John was not so much concerned about relating the facts of our Lord's ministry— that had already been done. John was concerned rather about giving those facts meaning, helping his readers see their spiritual significance. This becomes apparent already from the way in which he begins. Outside of class you might want to read the first chapter or two of each of the synoptic gospels and compare them with **John 1:1–18.** This section of John is called the prolog because it is an interpretive introduction to the entire gospel. In it John introduces key words, ideas, and themes that he will develop in the chapters that follow.

1. John starts his gospel with the words "In the beginning." What other book of the Bible begins the same way? Why is John drawing our attention to that book?

2. One of the great themes of John's prolog is that Jesus is the Word of God. What significant statements does John make about Jesus as the Word

of God in **1:1–4?**

3. How do **Genesis 1:1, 3, 6, 9, 11; Psalm 33:6, 9;** and **Isaiah 55:10–11** help us to understand the first three verses of the prolog?

4. The fourth gospel begins and ends with *life* (**1:4** and **20:31**). Life was a constant theme of Jesus' proclamation (**3:16; 5:40; 10:10; 17:2**). We will have occasion to look at the concept of *life* more than once in the gospel of John. This much needs to be said at the outset: life and Jesus are intimately linked together. He is life. We can have real life only by believing in Jesus. This life shines as a beacon of light, calling people to faith.

In **1:5,** John calls Jesus that light, but then points out that "the darkness has not understood it." The Greek word translated here as "understood" can also mean "overcome." Perhaps John intended to imply both meanings. In spite of the rejection Jesus experienced by the majority of people in His day and in spite of His rejection by many today, what will never happen to Jesus, the light of the world?

5. John the Baptizer was a very popular preacher (**Mark 1:4–5**). Many people thought that he might be the Messiah. But in what ways was Jesus uniquely different from John the Baptizer (**John 1:6–8**)? What did John testify about Jesus (**1:15**)?

6. God created all people. He is Lord of all, even of those who do not realize or acknowledge His lordship. But according to **John 1:12–13,** who only are God's children and how do they become that? See also what St. Paul has to say in **Romans 8:15** and **Galatians 4:4–5.**

7. In the Old Testament, God manifested His glory as a presence visible in a cloud (Exodus 40:34–35). During their wilderness wanderings and their early years in Canaan before the temple was built, God's glory dwelt among His people in the tabernacle, or tent of meeting. Two of God's characteristics that are mentioned repeatedly in the Old Testament are *unfailing love* and *faithfulness*. The corresponding Greek New Testament terms are *grace* and *truth*. Reread **John 1:1–3, 14.** How does John draw on the above-mentioned Old Testament images in **1:14** (the Greek for "made His dwelling among us" is related to the word *tabernacle*)?

8. Moses was one of the central figures in the Old Testament. God communicated with Moses in very special situations. Through Moses God also spoke to His people. It was Moses whom God chose to lead His people out of captivity into a life of freedom. As you recall the ministry and message of Moses, what similarities and what profound differences do you see between Moses and Jesus **(1:16–18)?**

The Witness of John the Baptizer (John 1:19–34)

Read **John 1:19–34.**

1. John identified Jesus as "the Lamb of God, who takes away the sin of the world" **(1:29).** Compare John's symbolism with these passages from the Old Testament: **Genesis 22:8; Exodus 12:3, 5–7, 23; Isaiah 53:7.** Consider also **1 Corinthians 5:7** and **Revelation 5:6–13.**

2. How does the baptism with which Jesus baptizes differ from the baptism of John **(John 1:26, 33; Matthew 3:11)?** John's experience at Jesus' baptism led to a confession and an action. What were they **(1:34)?**

The First Disciples (John 1:35–51)

1. Read **John 1:35–51.** What was it that convinced Andrew that Jesus was the Messiah?

2. As a result of their contact with Jesus, Andrew and Philip became disciples and missionaries. What was their message and what was their strategy for action?

The Word for Us

1. People have speculated, argued, and debated about what God is like. They have tried to represent Him in pictures and statues. They have drawn conclusions about God's nature from what happens in their personal lives and in the world. Christianity says that Jesus put an end to the need for such speculating. He has made God known to us. What Jesus did in person while He was on earth He now does through the Word recorded in the Bible and His Spirit, who opens our eyes to the truth in Scripture. What has Jesus revealed to you about God? What is the most important truth about God that your relationship to Jesus has helped you discover?

2. Many religions that have appealed to people in the past and some that are gaining popularity today, including some Eastern religions, teach that the material world is basically evil. According to these religions, the body is the prison of the soul. People must strive through a variety of means—prayer, diet, fasting, meditation, poverty—to escape the physical world in which they live. In contrast, Christianity declares that God became a human being in Jesus Christ. He had a body as physical and material as ours. What implications does that have for the way we view ourselves and the world we inhabit? How are we to value our created bodies and God's created world?

3. John calls Jesus "the true light that gives light to every man" **(John 1:9)**. What has Jesus brought to light in you or for you that you otherwise would not have been aware of?

4. What do you think it means to witness for Jesus? How do your ideas of witnessing compare with what Andrew and Philip did **(1:41–46)?** Is there anything you can learn from them?

Closing

Sing or read together "Savior of the Nations, Come."

Savior of the nations, come,
Show Yourself the virgin's son.
Marvel, heaven, wonder, earth,
That our God chose such a birth.

No man's pow'r of mind or blood
But the Spirit of our God
Made the Word of God be flesh,
Woman's offspring, pure and fresh.

God the Father was His source,
Back to God He ran His course.
Into hell His road went down,
Back then to His throne and crown.

Father's equal, You will win
Vict'ries for us over sin.
Might eternal, make us whole;
Heal our ills of flesh and soul.

Glory to the Father sing,
Glory to the Son, our king,
Glory to the Spirit be
Now and through eternity.

Lesson 2

Miraculous Signs (John 2)

Theme Verse

"This, the first of His miraculous signs, Jesus performed at Cana in Galilee. He thus revealed His glory, and His disciples put their faith in Him" (**John 2:11**).

Goal

That we might understand the purpose of Jesus' miraculous signs—to show His dominion over earthly powers and even over sin, death, and the devil.

What's Going On Here

Perhaps as you read you might notice the sharp contrast John draws between the marriage at Cana and the cleansing of the temple. On the surface, the wedding at Cana and the temple episode seem so different from one another. The one is set in a tiny village in the north of Palestine; the other, in the capital city of Jerusalem in the south. The first takes place in a social setting, a wedding; the other, in a very religious locale, the temple. In the first we see our Lord in a festive mood; in the second, He is angry. What is the connection between these two events? Since John tells us that he was selective in what he recorded and that he left out many things that Jesus did (**20:30** and **21:25**) what may have been his purpose for including these two accounts and for putting them together as he did?

Apparently John saw these two occurrences as embracing our Lord's entire ministry and purpose in coming to earth. Jesus began His ministry among the common people of Galilee and, according to the synoptic gospels, Galilee was the locale of most of His ministry. But the climax, the crucifixion and resurrection, occurred in Jerusalem, and is already introduced in the account of the cleansing of the temple (2:19–22). In relating these two episodes as he does, John accomplishes more than drawing our attention to the two main areas in which our Lord's ministry occurred. He introduces many of its key components: Jesus' miracles or, to use John's favorite term, "miraculous signs"; His concern for ordinary, common people; His conflict with the church leaders; His enjoyment of life; His mission to all mankind; His awareness that Messiahship would include death; and His certainty that beyond death there would be the resurrection.

The Wedding at Cana (John 2:1–11)

In Palestine a wedding was a very special occasion. It was not a brief ceremony followed by a short reception for the guests, after which the bride and groom hurried off on a honeymoon. Instead, after the wedding the bridal couple was escorted through the streets of the town to their new home, where a week of celebration followed. It was during this extended wedding reception that Jesus revealed His glory by rescuing the newlyweds from a rather embarrassing situation. They had underestimated the amount of wine they would need for the celebration. Or perhaps unexpected guests had shown up. Whatever the reason, there was a need, and Jesus, who never counted it a crime to be happy, came to the rescue.

But there is more to this episode than appears on the surface. John refers to what Jesus did as "the first of His *miraculous signs*" (2:11). What does he mean by that? Why did Jesus make such a large amount of wine? What is the meaning of the statement of the steward in 2:10?

The Cleansing of the Temple (John 2:12–25)

You can tell a lot about a person from what makes him angry. It doesn't take much to make some of us lose our temper. Our emotions lie close to the surface. Often even little things trigger a sudden outburst. Was Jesus like that? Although you may be familiar with His driving the money changers from the temple, you may never have thought of anger as part of Jesus' personality. Yet He *was* angry—and in the temple of all places! What could have been the cause? Why did Jesus act as He did? He created quite a scene. The leaders of the temple wanted to know what right He had to upset the business they saw as necessary for the orderly operation of the Lord's house. They wanted a miraculous sign. He gave them a sign, one which neither they nor His own disciple understood, at least not then. On what occasion did the comment about the miraculous sign about the three-day temple rebuilding come back to "haunt" Jesus?

Searching the Scriptures

The Wedding at Cana (John 2:1–11)

Read **John 2:1–11.**

1. Where did Jesus perform His first miracle? What was the occasion? What prompted Him to act? What does this tell you about Jesus?

2. In **2:4** Jesus addressed His mother as "dear woman." Read **John 19:26,** where Jesus addresses her again with this term. How had the situation changed? The response of Jesus to His mother in **2:4** sounds very condescending. The expression "My time" occurs several times in John's gospel. It does not always have the same meaning. Compare **7:30; 8:20; 12:23, 27; 13:1;** and **17:1.** Go back to **John 19:26.** Had Jesus' time now come?

3. Jesus made wine out of water that was contained in large jars used for purification rites. Why do you think that fact is mentioned by John? How does Jesus' statement about "new wine" in **Mark 2:22** help us to understand the deeper meaning of the reference made by the master of the banquet about "the choice wine"? To what do both expressions refer?

The Cleansing of the Temple (John 2:12–25)

1. What did the money changers and sellers of animals have to do with the temple worship? Remember: sacrifice was a central part of Old Testament worship.

2. Why did Jesus become so angry? Look at the parallel accounts in the other gospels to get additional clues, especially **Matthew 21:13; Mark 11:17; Luke 19:46.**

3. Most people did not understand the message that the "miraculous signs" of Jesus were meant to convey. Neither did they always catch the real meaning of what He said. How did the Jews in the temple misunderstand Jesus **(2:18–20)?** See also **Mark 14:58** and **15:29.**

The Word for Us

1. The first miracle that Jesus performed was done in a simple, family setting. It was there that He "revealed His glory" **(2:11).** How do we act at home? What do we display to our families? Are we, like Jesus, responsive to the feelings and the needs of those closest to us? or is it easier to save our kindness for strangers and friends?

2. On more than one occasion the gospel writers tell us about Jesus being at festive celebrations—weddings, dinners, banquets. He was glad to be with people who were having a good time. How about you? Does your faith hinder or help you to enjoy life?

3. What does the fact that Jesus became angry say to you about anger? Is anger wrong? Is it a sin for us to become angry? How do you handle anger? How does your faith help you handle your anger?

Closing

Sing or read together the words of Christina G. Rossetti from "Love Came Down at Christmas."

Worship we the Godhead,
  Love incarnate, Love divine;
Worship we our Jesus:
  But wherewith for sacred sign?

Love shall be our token,
  Love be yours and love be mine,
Love to God and all men,
  Love for plea and gift and sign.

Lesson 3

Two Who Misunderstood (John 3:1–4:42)

Theme Verse

" 'You are Israel's teacher,' said Jesus, 'and do you not understand these things?' " (**John 3:10**).

Goal

That we might understand that Jesus' message was clear: salvation comes only through faith in His redeeming work. Yet consistently throughout the New Testament, people misunderstood His message.

What's Going On Here

In the prolog John said: "The light shines in the darkness, but the darkness has not understood it" (**1:5**). The readings for this session are a commentary on that verse. They tell us about two people who had this one thing in common: they missed the point—at least initially—of what Jesus was saying to them. In this respect they are representative of the majority of the people with whom Jesus came in contact. Most people did not fully understand what Jesus said because they did not fully understand who Jesus was. The two go hand in hand. Because the two people we meet in this lesson did not really know who it was that they were talking to, they did not know how to understand what He said to them.

Except for the fact that they both missed the point of what Jesus said to them, they are strikingly different. We know the name of one but not of the other. Nicodemus was a Jew. He was both a Pharisee and a respected member of the Sanhedrin. The other was a woman of Samaria whose immoral life made her an outcast from her own community. Nicodemus intentionally sought out Jesus and came to Him at night. The Samaritan woman met Jesus quite by accident when she came to the well to draw water in the middle of the day. The one approached Jesus with respect, the other with antagonism. We don't find out what effect Jesus' conversation had on Nicodemus, but we know that the Samaritan woman became a changed person.

The Interview with Nicodemus (John 3:1–21)

Nicodemus came to Jesus at night (3:2), perhaps because he did not want anyone else to know about his visit. He was a Pharisee, and most of the Pharisees hated Jesus. But he had to find out about Jesus for himself.

Like every pious Jew, Nicodemus was eagerly waiting for God to establish His kingdom among His people. As Nicodemus and Jesus talked about that, Jesus said that the only way into God's kingdom was for a person to be "born *again*" (3:3; emphasis added). Nicodemus understood that literally and was utterly confused. But Jesus was speaking of a spiritual rebirth. In actual fact, the word He used can mean not only "again" but also "from above." Undoubtedly, our Lord had both meanings in mind. To enter God's kingdom one must have a radical spiritual rebirth and that rebirth is something that can only come from above. It is something that only God can accomplish. He does it by the power of His Spirit through Baptism.

Nicodemus did not understand how such a thing could happen. Jesus reminded him that there are many things we don't understand but that does not keep them from being true. As an illustration, He mentioned the wind (3:8), which is something more than it appears to be. The Greek word for *wind* is also the word used for *spirit*. Jesus was saying that God's Spirit, like the wind, operates even though we may not be able to explain how. God's Spirit is powerful and brings about the rebirth that Jesus said was necessary for entrance into God's kingdom. Jesus told Nicodemus that he can know that this is true because the one speaking to him is God's own Son, sent to establish God's kingdom and make eternal life available to all people.

Jesus and the Woman at the Well (4:1–42)

On the long walk from Judea to Galilee—Palestine is about 120 miles from south to north—Jesus stopped near the town of Sychar in Samaria. It was noon. He was tired and sat down near the village well while the disciples went into town to buy food—in itself a surprising act, since Jews ordinarily refused to have any contact with Samaritans. Apparently Jesus' influence was beginning to have an effect on them. When a woman came to the well to draw water, Jesus asked her for a drink. This was her chance, she thought, to get even with one of those haughty Jews who despised her people. Besides, a Jewish man normally would not even speak to a woman in public. She decided He must be desperate for a drink. She answered Him with a put-down **(4:9)**. But Jesus was not put off by her reply. Instead, to her amazement, He offered her "living" water **(4:10)**. She misunderstood, because the word Jesus used *(living)* can also mean "stream" or "running" water. She sarcastically replied that there was no other source of water anywhere around except for this well, which had been dug by Jacob nearly 2,000 years earlier. Then she asked, "Are You greater than our father Jacob" **(4:12)?** Before her encounter with Jesus ended, she would answer her own question. It took some doing, but Jesus finally got through to her. She came to see who Jesus really was, and in the process she also came to see herself for who she really was. Her life had been a scenario fit for an X-rated movie. She left her water jar behind and rushed back to town with the news of her discovery. The villagers who came out to see the person she told them about invited Jesus to remain with them. So for two days Jesus stayed in Sychar, talking and teaching. When He finally left, the Samaritans knew from firsthand experience that Jesus was the Savior of the world.

Searching the Scriptures

The Interview with Nicodemus (John 3:1–21)

1. Who were the Pharisees mentioned so many times in the gospel? (Besides the gospels themselves, a source of information is a Bible dictionary.)

2. Why did Nicodemus come to Jesus "at night" **(3:2)?** What is significant about the night? (See **1:5; 3:19; 13:30.**)

3. The idea of rebirth or being born again runs through the entire New Testament. Check **2 Corinthians 5:17; Galatians 6:15; Titus 3:5; 1 Peter 1:3, 23.** What did Nicodemus mean by asking "How can a man be

born when he is old?"

4. The account of Moses and the serpent referred to in **3:14–15** is in **Numbers 21:4–9.** What is John referring to when he says "so the Son of Man must be *lifted up?*" See **John 8:28** and **John 12:32.** The same expression is used in **Acts 2:33; 5:31;** and **Philippians 2:9.** To what does it refer in these passages?

5. **John 3:16** is probably the best-known verse of the New Testament. Take a few minutes to think about it. What does it tell you about God?

The Woman at the Well (John 4:1–42)

1. Jesus was concerned about *all* people, regardless of race or gender. He was not bound by the conventional restrictions of His day, which would have compelled Him to remain aloof from certain individuals. How do **4:9** and **27** emphasize this?

2. Why do you think the woman brought up the controversy about the proper place to worship **(4:20)**? In the ancient world you had to go to the temple dedicated to a specific god in order to worship that god. What did Jesus mean by His response, "True worshipers will worship the Father in spirit and truth" **(4:23)**?

3. It is possible to see the gradual change in the woman's attitude toward Jesus by the expressions she uses in speaking to Him or about Him. Notice the progression in **4:9, 11, 19, 25,** and **29.** How did her attitude change?

The Word for Us

1. Nicodemus seemed to want to change. His question, "How can a man be born when he is old?" may be the desperate cry of one who wants to be different from what he is but who knows that he cannot change himself. Often we feel trapped by personal problems or weaknesses we cannot seem to change. Why can't we change? What resources for change do we have as Christians that others don't have?

2. **John 3:16** says that whoever believes in Jesus shall not perish but have eternal life. We talk a lot about "believing in Jesus." It is probably mentioned in just about every sermon you hear. If somebody asked you: "What does it mean to believe in Jesus?" what would you say?

3. Jesus came to break down the barriers that separate us from one another. He made no distinctions. He accepted everyone regardless of race, gender, financial, or social status. God's love is for all people. How do we make that evident by the way we treat people?

Closing

Sing or read together "God Loved the World So that He Gave."

God loved the world so that He gave
His only Son the lost to save
That all who would in Him believe
Should everlasting life receive.

Christ Jesus is the ground of faith,
Who was made flesh and suffered death;
All who confide in Christ alone
Are built on this chief cornerstone.

If you are sick, if death is near,
This truth your troubled heart can cheer:
Christ Jesus saves your soul from death;
That is the firmest ground of faith.

Be of good cheer, for God's own Son
Forgives all sins which you have done;
You're justified by Jesus' blood;
Baptized, you have the highest good.

Glory to God the Father, Son,
And Holy Spirit, Three in One!
To You, O blessed Trinity,
Be praise now and eternally!

Lesson 4

You Can't Do That!
(John 4:43–5:47)

Theme Verse

"For this reason the Jews tried all the harder to kill Him; not only was He breaking the Sabbath, but He was even calling God His own Father, making Himself equal with God" **(John 5:18).**

Goal

That we may be encouraged by the faith of the official **(4:43–54)** and by the words of Jesus **(5:19–47)** to share the Good News of salvation with those we come in contact with in our everyday life.

What's Going On Here

After interrupting His journey for two days at the request of the villagers of Sychar, Jesus continued north to Galilee, returning to the site of His first miracle. Word of what He had done in Jerusalem preceded Him. He had been in Cana only a short time when one of Herod's officers traveled south from Capernaum to plead with Jesus for help for his son, who was near death. Jesus rebuked the man but the official would not give up. It was only when Jesus assured him that his son would live that the man started for home. On the way his servants met him with the good news that the son was living; he had made a dramatic recovery at the exact moment when Jesus assured him his son would live. John says this was the second miraculous sign that Jesus did. The official understood the sign and responded not simply with gratitude, but with faith in Jesus as Savior.

The faith of the official is set in sharp contrast to the reaction of the Jews to Jesus' healing of a crippled man in Jerusalem **(5:1–18).** The miracle took place near a pool, which was surrounded by a throng of people with various maladies who believed that at certain times when the water of the pool stirred, whoever was first to enter the water was restored to health. Jesus was touched by the plight of a man, who had been an invalid for 38 years. Jesus healed him and instructed him to pick up the mat he had been lying on and go home. What should have caused a joyful celebration instead caused trouble. When the Jews saw the man carrying his mat, they accused him of working on the Sabbath, a day reserved for rest. The extraordinary circumstances made no difference to them. Their legalistic approach to life made it impossible to allow for exceptions. When they discovered that the man had, in effect, been told to break the Sabbath by Jesus, their anger knew no limit. In their view, He had desecrated the temple on a previous visit to Jerusalem; now He was encouraging people to disregard God's Law. Then, when they confronted Jesus over the matter, He made claims they considered to be wild and blasphemous. Jesus claimed God as His Father and that He and God were one **(5:19–20).** He referred to Himself as God's Son, who was acting in accord with the will of His Father. In essence, He was saying that He had God's approval to break the Sabbath. He went on to say that God sent Him into the world and that the life of God was in Him. Not only did He have the life of God, but He will use it to call back into life those who are dead **(5:24).**

The claims that Jesus made were utterly astounding. It took complete self-assurance and courage to say the things that He did, knowing the attitude and the power of His antagonists. There were only two options open to them. Either they could accept Jesus' assertions as true or pronounce Him a blasphemer deserving of death.

Searching the Scriptures

Acts of Healing (John 4:43–5:18)

1. How did the official who came to Jesus show that he believed Jesus? Compare the man's reaction in **4:50, 53.** What was it that the official believed in?

2. Try to imagine the scene by the pool. It may be difficult to picture what it must have been like to be sick or an invalid during the time that Jesus lived. There were no hospitals, clinics, nursing homes, or facilities for treating people with physical and emotional problems. All the people

that today find help in institutions were out in the community—in homes, even in the streets. Again and again such people swarmed around Jesus, seeking help. Sometimes we may try to avoid the infirm because their condition makes us uncomfortable or makes us feel guilty. Jesus not only accepted them when they came to Him, but He took the initiative in helping them **(5:6)**. Why do you think Jesus asked the invalid whether he wanted to be healed? Wasn't that self-evident?

3. Like other people we have met so far in John's gospel, what did the invalid do **(5:15)**?

4. In what way does the statement of Jesus in **5:17** apply to the accusation that He is guilty of breaking the Sabbath?

The Discourse to the Jews (John 5:19–47)

1. According to **5:19,** how did Jesus identify Himself? What did He claim that He was doing?

2. What are the "greater things" that Jesus refers to in **5:20?** According to **5:20–21** what power and authority does Jesus have? Who only has eternal life and is free from God's judgment **(5:24)?**

3. Who were the "dead" referred to in **5:25?**

4. Jesus was conscious that He was not acting on His own. What did He claim as authorization for all He does **(5:30)?**

Jesus claimed John the Baptizer as one of His witnesses **(5:33).** What did John say about Jesus **(1:29–36; 3:26–30)?**

5. According to **5:39–40** what is possible even for those who study the Bible diligently? What is the key to a correct understanding of the Scriptures? What is the purpose of Scripture?

6. What did Jesus mean when He said, "Your accuser is Moses, on whom your hopes are set" **(5:45)?** What are the writings of Moses that Jesus mentions in **5:47** and why does the refusal to believe them result in the refusal to believe the words of Jesus?

The Word for Us

1. There are those in the church who say that it is the church's mission to be concerned about the whole person. That means working to relieve physical distress, as well as social and economic injustices that afflict people. There are others who say that the business of the church is only to preach the Gospel. The church should be concerned about people's souls, not their bodies. What do you say? What does the ministry of Jesus indicate about the way in which He might have answered the question?

2. Try to imagine yourself as one of the Jewish leaders listening to Jesus. How do you think you would have reacted to the things He said? Do people today react as strongly to our message of salvation?

3. Probably this is not the first time that you have read the gospel of John. Are there any statements of our Lord in **John 5:19–47** that are particularly important to you personally?

Closing

Sing or read together the words of "O God, O Lord of Heaven and Earth."

O God, O Lord of heav'n and earth,
    Your living finger never wrote
    That life should be an aimless mote,
A deathward drift from futile birth.
Your Word meant life triumphant hurled
In splendor through Your broken world;
Since light awoke and life began,
You made for us a holy plan.

In blind revolt we would not see
    That rebel wills wrought death and night.
    We seized and used in fear and spite
Your wondrous gift of liberty.
We walled us in this house of doom,
Where death had royal scope and room,
Until Your servant, Prince of Peace,
Broke down its walls for our release.

You came into our hall of death,
    O Christ, to breathe our poisoned air,
    To drink for us the deep despair
That strangled our reluctant breath.
How beautiful the feet that trod
The road to bring good news from God!
How beautiful the feet that bring
Good tidings of our saving king!

O Spirit, who did once restore
    The Church that it might yet recall
    The bringer of good news to all:
Breathe on Your cloven Church once more
That in these gray and latter days
There may be those whose life is praise,
Each life a high doxology
Unto the holy Trinity.

Lesson 5

Bread Like You Never Had Before
(John 6)

Theme Verse

"I am the bread of life. He who comes to Me will never go hungry, and he who believes in Me will never be thirsty" **(John 6:35).**

Goal

In this session, we learn that Jesus, the Bread of life, feeds us with His Word, nourishing us so that we can share this life-giving Bread with others.

What's Going On Here

Chapter 6 follows the same basic pattern as the previous chapter. Both begin with a miracle, which then becomes an opportunity for Jesus to begin a longer discourse on the meaning of His miracles or ministry. In **chapter 5** the healing of the crippled man led to a confrontation with the Jews in which Jesus defended His working on the Sabbath and declared that He is God's Son. In **chapter 6** the feeding of the 5,000 is followed by a long discussion with the Jews in which Jesus reveals Himself to be the Bread of life.

John begins **chapter 6** by noting that "the Jewish Passover Feast was near" **(6:4).** In light of the discourse that follows, John's observation seems to have special significance. The Lord's Supper is the Christian Passover, and Jesus is the Christian *Paschal Lamb.* The entire chapter, while not specifically naming the Lord's Supper, revolves around a special feeding: Jesus the *Bread of life.* We eat His flesh and do not hunger; we drink His blood and do not thirst (see **6:35**).

A large crowd of people followed Jesus into the hills, where He had gone with His disciples (6:3–5). Jesus felt a responsibility for the crowd and asked His disciples where they were going to buy food for all the people. Philip expressed despair at the prospect (6:7), but Andrew found a boy who had a small lunch (6:8–9). It wasn't much, but Jesus is able to do wonders with even the least we offer Him. Jesus miraculously multiplied the boy's meager supplies, so that everyone had all they could eat, and there was more left over than they started with. Realizing what Jesus had done, the crowd decided to make Him king (6:15). With Him as their leader, they would have no need for such things as Social Security, Medicare, or food stamps. But Jesus had more than a mere earthly kingdom in mind. He would have nothing to do with their plans. Mark tells us that Jesus sent His disciples away (Mark 6:45), perhaps so they would not be influenced by the attitude of the crowd. Then, after He had convinced the crowd to disband, Jesus went into the hills to be by Himself. Later that night He came walking to the disciples on the Sea of Galilee as they struggled to get their boat to shore against a strong wind. (The Sea of Galilee was also called the Sea of Tiberias, the Lake of Gennesaret, and the Sea of Kinnereth.) Jesus calmed His frightened disciples by saying "It is I" (6:20); it was in this same way that God identified Himself to a frightened Moses when He appeared to him in the burning bush (Exodus 3:14). John wants us to realize that Jesus and God are one.

The next day when the crowd realized that Jesus had left during the night, they went by boat across the sea to Him (6:24). The boats they used may have been blown in by the storm or may have been sent by God as another miracle. John doesn't elaborate. Jesus was not surprised to see them—He knew why they had come. He tried to tell them that He wants disciples, not just sensation-seeking followers. But they were not interested in what He was saying. They wanted Him for what He could do for them. Jesus told them not to work just for those things that fill their stomachs (6:27). The word *work* prompted them to ask what kind of work God wanted them to do (6:28). The answer of Jesus was that the *work* of God is that they believe in Him, the Savior God has sent. They asked Jesus for a sign to prove that He had, in truth, come from God as He claimed. Moses had given the Israelites of his day bread from heaven in the wilderness as a sign. Could Jesus match that sign? Jesus not only could match it; He offered them something infinitely superior, a bread that would give them life (6:29–34). Just as the Samaritan woman misunderstood when Jesus offered her *living water*, so the Jews here misunderstood Jesus' offer of *life-giving bread.*

Their misunderstanding gave Jesus the opening to clarify what He meant. He is the *Bread of life*. He can satisfy man's deepest hunger. All one has to do is believe in Him. God's sumptuous, satisfying meal is ours for the taking. God sent Jesus to do His will. What is God's will? It is not first of all, as the Jews imagined, what God wants *from* people but what God wants *for* people. God's will is that everyone should believe that Jesus is His Son and in believing receive eternal life **(6:40).**

The crowd could not accept this concept. They knew Jesus' earthly parents. After all, He grew up not far from where they were. They saw Him as a carpenter from Nazareth. This dialog was a watershed in Jesus' ministry. At this point some of His followers who were looking for an earthly savior began to defect. The desertion that began here culminated in His complete aloneness on the cross, where He felt Himself forsaken even by God. At this time, however, all was not yet gloom. Peter spoke for the Twelve **(6:68).** No, they would not leave Him. He was their life. There was no one else for them to turn to. Only Jesus could offer them eternal life. Only He is "the Holy One of God" **(6:69).**

Searching the Scriptures
The Feeding of the 5,000 (John 6:1–15)

1. According to **6:2,** what motivated many people to clamor after Jesus?

2. Andrew was not one of the inner circle of disciples to whom Jesus turned at crucial times. He does not figure prominently in the book of Acts. Yet he can be a model for each of us. His greatness lay in whom he brought to Jesus. In this instance he brought a youngster who had the ingredients with which Jesus could perform a miracle. Whom else had Andrew brought to Jesus **(1:40–42)?**

3. Does the description of the feeding of the 5,000 in **6:11** remind you of another feeding described in the gospels? Think about it in connection with the discussion Jesus has later in the chapter in which He speaks

about eating His flesh and drinking His blood.

4. The Jews could not help but see a parallel between what Jesus accomplished and what God did through two of their heroes in the Old Testament. See **2 Kings 4:42–44; Exodus 16; Numbers 11.** What was the difference between the food God provided for His people in the Old Testament and the food that Jesus spoke of?

Jesus Walking on the Water (John 6:16–21)

The episode of Jesus walking on the sea concludes with a statement by Him that was meant not only for the disciples in the boat but for His disciples in all ages **(6:20).**

When Jesus said to His disciples, "It is I," He was saying more than we probably realize. He was making a claim and an identification that is not apparent in our translations. The Greek reads literally, "He says to them, *I am.*" His words could not fail to remind people familiar with Scripture of **Exodus 3:14.** What was Jesus saying about Himself?

Discourse on the Bread of Life (John 6:22–71)

1. What did Jesus mean when He said, "You are looking for Me, not because you saw miraculous signs but because you ate the loaves and had your fill" **(6:26)?**

2. What is the point of **6:27?** If you were to put it in your own words, what would you say?

3. The religion of many of the people at this time (and even today!) was based on works. They were conscious and concerned about doing the things God commanded. Therefore they asked Jesus what works God demanded. What was His startling reply (6:29)? Then what was their reply (6:30)?

4. **John 6:35–40** are among the greatest verses in the entire gospel because of what they tell us about Jesus. List the things this passage says to you.

5. What did Jesus say about Himself in **6:46?**

6. Notice how similar the wording of **John 6:53–57** is to that of **Matthew 26:26–29.** How do Jesus' words in the Matthew passage help us to understand Jesus' words in the John passage?

7. What did the Jews mean when they said in **6:60,** "This is a hard teaching"?

8. What does **6:63–65** tell us about the all-important work of the Holy Spirit?

The Word for Us

1. In this portion of the gospel Jesus claimed great authority by His acts, and by His words claimed to be God's salvation and the way of eternal life. The Jews found this "hard" to believe. Many today still find this hard to

believe. What is difficult to accept about the claim of Christ to be Savior? Why is it so difficult for some to believe? What can you do for a person who is struggling with doubt? How do you deal with your own doubts?

2. Many people who followed Jesus during His lifetime were eager to support Him as long as He gave them what they wanted. They really wished to use Him, not to be used by Him. In what way can this be a temptation for each of us?

Closing

Sing or read together "Lord Jesus Christ, Life-Giving Bread."

Lord Jesus Christ, life-giving bread,
    May I in grace possess You.
Let me with holy food be fed,
    In hunger I address You.
Prepare me well for You, O Lord,
And, humbly by my prayer implored,
    Give me Your grace and mercy.

O bread of heav'n, my soul's delight,
    For full and free remission
I come with prayer before Your sight
    In sorrow and contrition.
Your righteousness, Lord, cover me
That I receive You worthily,
    Assured of Your full pardon.

I do not merit favor, Lord,
    My weight of sin would break me;
In all my guilty heart's discord,
    O Lord, do not forsake me.
In my distress this comforts me
That You receive me graciously,
    O Christ, my Lord of mercy!

Lesson 6

Hostility Grows (John 7–8)

Theme Verse

" 'If you were Abraham's children,' said Jesus, 'then you would do the things Abraham did. As it is, you are determined to kill Me, a man who has told you the truth that I heard from God' " (**John 8:39–40**).

Goal

In this session, we learn that Jesus does not fit into our preconceived notions of a savior. He is the truth, He speaks the truth, He lived the truth; and sometimes, in our sinful state, the truth hurts. But the truth of His death and resurrection heals our wounded souls.

What's Going On Here

It is one of the ironies of our Lord's life that, although He came to proclaim peace, He was pursued by constant controversy. Again in this part of the gospel we see Him in conflict with the religious authorities. It was in the autumn, during the time of the Festival of Tabernacles (Booths), at which the Jews celebrated the gathering of their crops and commemorated the 40 years their ancestors wandered in the wilderness. Jesus went to Jerusalem for the festival. About the middle of the weeklong festival, He began to teach the crowds that had come to the temple. They were amazed at His learning. He was, after all, a common laborer. He had not studied under any rabbi. Where did His knowledge come from? It came from God, He said. Jesus had made that claim before and had drawn the hostility of the Pharisees because of it. There was no way they would let Him get away with it this time, not in front of all the pilgrims who were in Jerusalem for the festival. They sent a contingent of the temple police to arrest Him

(7:32). The Pharisees were furious when the officers returned empty-handed. Even the soldiers were impressed with Jesus. They had never heard anyone speak with such authority and burning conviction. The Pharisees were incensed and abused the officers verbally. Only uninformed, "common" people believe Jesus' teachings, they point out (7:47–49). Perhaps not. One of their own number, Nicodemus, a member of the Sanhedrin who had come to Jesus by night, made a timid attempt to defend Jesus (7:51). They set upon him with a sarcastic taunt that did not really reply to the objection he had raised but did succeed in silencing him.

Chapter 8 begins with the story of the woman caught in the act of adultery. Because section **7:53–8:11** does not appear in the oldest manuscripts most modern translations place it in a footnote. Some commentators theorize that although the early manuscripts do not include this story, it probably really happened, but because it was so gracious toward the adulterous woman, for many years men were afraid to tell it. This story sets in sharpest relief the difference between the Pharisees and Jesus.

Jesus claimed to be the Light of the world (8:12); thus implying that the Pharisees were living in darkness. He made a clear, bold claim to be God. He promised to lead those who believe in Him into the truth and to make them free. The Pharisees responded that as Abraham's descendants, they were slaves to no one (8:33). Jesus replied Abraham's descendants would not seek to kill Him; therefore the devil is their father (8:34–38; 44). That did not win Him any friends! When He challenged the Pharisees to prove His guilt, they changed the subject (8:46–48). He responded that whoever believes in Him will never die. His opponents think they have Him trapped. They exclaim that Abraham died; the prophets died. Is Jesus greater than their father Abraham (8:53)? Who does He think He is? This is what He had been trying to tell them all along. He tried once more. He told them as emphatically as He could, "Before Abraham was born, I am!" (8:58). They finally understood, but it was more than they could tolerate. They were through talking. They recognized blasphemy and they knew how to handle blasphemers—"they picked up stones to stone Him."

Searching the Scriptures

Jesus at the Feast of Tabernacles (John 7)

1. Why did Jesus' brothers want him to go to Jerusalem? Why do you think it was hard for them to understand what Jesus was doing?

2. The Pharisees repeatedly demanded that Jesus prove His teaching was from God as He claimed. According to **7:17** how should we test the truth of Jesus' teaching?

3. Jesus snared the legalistic Pharisees in an argument of their own making. What did He refer to in order to show them that they do not keep the Law **(7:19–24)?**

4. What was a popular belief about the Messiah **(7:27)?** How did this belief seem to argue against Jesus' claim to be the Messiah?

5. Jesus continued to be misunderstood. He talked about leaving and going to a place where the Jews would not be able to follow **(7:33–34)**. What was He talking about? What is meant by "our people [who] live scattered among the Greeks" **(7:35)?**

6. **Verse 39** is a very significant passage. What does it tell us about the relationship of the Holy Spirit to Jesus?

The Woman Caught in Adultery (John 8:1–11)

1. Were the Pharisees concerned about this woman? Why had they brought her to Jesus?

2. Why were the older accusers the first ones to leave (8:9)?

3. Look at Jesus' response to the woman in 8:11. What did He tell her?

The Witness of the Father (John 8:12–59)

1. **Verses 31–32** are packed with meaning. Look at them again. What do they tell us about discipleship?

2. What formal relationship were the Jews counting on and how did they try to use it to respond to Jesus' offer of freedom (8:33–41)?

3. How do you explain Jesus' statement in 8:51?

4. Few statements of Jesus are more staggering than that in 8:58. (See also 8:12: "*I am* the light of the world" and 8:24: "if you do not believe that *I am* the one I claim to be." [Emphasis added.]) Why did Jews try to stone Him?

The Word for Us

1. It is obvious from the way Jesus dealt with the woman caught in adultery that our Lord looked beyond the letter of God's Law to its inner intention. (See **Galatians 3:21–25**.) **Leviticus 20:10** demanded the woman's execution—yet Jesus did not condemn her. Why did He disregard the Law's demand for punishment—the Law's demand for the death of the woman? What did Jesus' handling of the woman indicate about His attitude toward the sinner? How is Jesus to be our example in dealing with those who have sinned?

2. Jesus says that if we continue in His Word we will know the truth and the truth will make us free **(8:32)**. We might be inclined to say with the Jews: "We are Abraham's descendants and have never been slaves of anyone. How can you say that we shall be set free?" **(8:33)**. Can you think of things that tend to enslave us and rob us of our freedom? How does the relationship we have with Christ through the Gospel help us to be free from these enslavements?

Closing

Sing or read together the words of "Christ Be My Leader."

Christ be my leader by night as by day;
Safe through the darkness, for He is the way.
Gladly I follow, my future His care;
Darkness is daylight when Jesus is there.

Christ be my teacher in age as in youth,
Drifting or doubting, for He is the truth.
Grant me to trust Him; though shifting as sand,
Doubt cannot daunt me; in Jesus I stand.

Christ be my savior in calm as in strife;
Death cannot hold me, for He is the life.
Nor darkness nor doubting nor sin and its stain
Can touch my salvation: with Jesus I reign.

(Text by Timothy Dudley-Smith. © 1964. Renewal 1992 by Hope Publishing Co., Carol Stream, IL 60188. All rights reserved. Used by permission.)

Lesson 7

The Shepherd and His Sheep (John 9–10)

Theme Verse

"I am the good shepherd. The good shepherd lays down His life for the sheep" **(John 10:11)**.

Goal

"All we like sheep have gone astray." In this session, we learn that only Jesus, the Good Shepherd can bring us back into the fold of God's family. Only Jesus can protect us from the evil one.

What's Going On Here

The Man Born Blind (John 9)

Chapter 9 narrates the sixth of the seven miraculous signs recorded by John in his gospel and the controversy that follows because of it. Once more Jesus gets in trouble with the Pharisees **(9:13–16)**. In giving sight to the man born blind Jesus had broken the Sabbath laws established by the Pharisees on two counts: first, by making clay to put on the man's eyes, He was guilty of working; second, it was forbidden to practice medicine on the Sabbath. According to their laws medical care could be administered only if a person's life was in danger, but even then only to keep the patient from getting worse, not to help him get better. Once again the question that dominates the controversy, and the one that John wants every one of his readers to answer is "Who is Jesus?" The question put to the blind man **(9:17)** comes to us too: "What have you to say about Him? It was your eyes He opened."

Jesus the Good Shepherd (John 10)

In the Old Testament God is often pictured as a shepherd and the children of Israel as His sheep. "You led Your people like a flock by the hand of Moses and Aaron" **(Psalm 77:20).** "He is our God and we are the people of His pasture, the flock under His care" **(Psalm 95:7).** "Hear us, O Shepherd of Israel, You who lead Joseph like a flock" **(Psalm 80:1).** The Messiah is also pictured as a shepherd. "He tends His flock like a shepherd: He gathers the lambs in His arms and carries them close to His heart; He gently leads those that have young" **(Isaiah 40:11).** The prophets refer to the leaders of Israel as its shepherds. "Woe to the shepherds who are destroying and scattering the sheep of My pasture" **(Jeremiah 23:1).** The most fearful indictment of the false shepherds of Israel is given in **Ezekiel 34.** Read this chapter in order to catch the full implication of what Jesus was saying both about Himself and about the religious leaders of His day when He referred to Himself as the Good Shepherd and when He talked about the hired hand who cares nothing for the sheep.

Searching the Scriptures
The Man Born Blind (John 9)

1. What was the popular belief in our Lord's day to account for any misfortune or tragedy that happened in a person's life **(9:2)?** See also **Luke 13:1–5.** How did Jesus respond to the question of His disciples **(9:3)?** What did Jesus mean in **9:4?** How is His statement applicable to us?

2. Jesus claimed (in **9:5**) to be "the light of the world." How does the miracle reported in **chapter 9** show that He is?

3. The Pharisees "were divided" over Jesus **(9:16).** What was this division about? This is not the first time such a division occurred. See **7:43.**

4. The Pharisees were not satisfied with the man's answer to their question **(9:17)**, so how did they try to discredit Jesus **(9:18–23)?**
What tactic did the Jews resort to in order to keep people from confessing Jesus to be the Messiah?

5. The Pharisees tried to lure the man who had been born blind into a theological debate, pressuring him to declare that Jesus had done wrong by helping him on the Sabbath. How did he neatly skirt their trap **(9:25)?** His answer is a good example of effective witnessing. What did he simply say?

6. Notice the progression in recognition and reaction to Jesus on the part of the man as seen in **9:11, 17, 36,** and **38.** Along with his physical sight, the man also received spiritual insight. Think about your own faith progression. How did you think about Jesus when you were a child? A teenager? Ten years ago? Last month? Today? Only the Holy Spirit can increase our faith, but sometimes we do our best to block His work. Where would you like to see your faith next year? in 10 years?

Jesus the Good Shepherd (John 10)
1. John states in **10:6** that the Jews did not understand what Jesus was saying in the preceding verses. What was it that He was saying about Himself and about those who believe in Him in **10:3–5?**

2. Jesus changed the figure of speech or analogy in **10:7.** To what did He compare Himself in that verse?

3. Who are the "thieves and robbers" referred to in **10:8?** How does Jesus differ from these marauders **(10:10–11)?** What do you learn about our Good Shepherd in **10:14–15?** What comfort do you find in **10:17–18, 27–29?**

4. To whom was Jesus referring in **10:16** when He spoke of "other sheep"?

5. What did Jesus mean when He said, "Do not believe me unless I do what my Father does" **(10:37)?**

6. The apostle John tried to make sure that his readers would realize the significance of John the Baptizer as well as the difference between John and Jesus. In **10:41** how did he restate and reinforce what he had previously said?

The Word for Us

1. Would you agree that affliction, pain, and disappointment can be avenues by which God leads us to His Word and helps us to help others? Can you share an experience—your own or someone else's—that helped you discover His presence?

2. We live in a world that tends to depersonalize people. Our name is often not as important as our number—Social Security, credit card, PIN, driver's license. We can be surrounded by people and yet be very much alone because our lives don't really touch or intersect. It is easy to feel that nobody knows us, that nobody cares about us. Does Jesus Christ speak to this condition of loneliness?

3. **Chapter 10** is a favorite source of selections to be read at funerals. Which verses do you think are the most meaningful for those who are grieving? Can you share with the group a time in your life when some part of this chapter had special meaning for you? What did it say to you then? Because of your experience, how might you encourage others in times of trouble?

Closing

Read or sing together the words of "Have No Fear, Little Flock."

Have no fear, little flock;
Have no fear, little flock,
   For the Father has chosen
   To give you the Kingdom;
Have no fear, little flock!

Have good cheer, little flock;
Have good cheer, little flock,
   For the Father will keep you
   In His love forever;
Have good cheer, little flock!

Praise the Lord high above;
Praise the Lord high above,
   For He stoops down to heal you,
   Uplift and restore you;
Praise the Lord high above.

Thankful hearts raise to God;
Thankful hearts raise to God,
   For He stays close beside you,
   In all things works with you;
Thankful hearts raise to God!

Lesson 8

The Resurrection
and the Life
(John 11)

Theme Verse

"I am the resurrection and the life. He who believes in Me will live, even though he dies; and whoever lives and believes in Me will never die" (**John 11:25–26**).

Goal

In this session, we learn that Jesus came to bring life. As we walk in faith, we are never alone, and we are strengthened by the Lord as we face the trials of life. But the life Jesus gives doesn't end at death; indeed that is when it begins in its fullness.

What's Going On Here

The raising of Lazarus from the dead was the last and the most astounding of the seven miraculous signs recorded by John. Like the other miraculous signs, this one was not really *seen* by all who actually observed it or were told about it. It did not force people to believe. On the contrary, in the case of the priests and the Pharisees, it hardened their resolve to get rid of Jesus. John makes it clear that Jesus was crucified because He performed works that were leading more and more people to believe that He was the Messiah. We need to remember that Jesus was not put to death because He was a good man or a courageous preacher or an irritating social critic—though He was all of these—but because He was the Son of God. John's initial witness stands true: "He was in the world, and ... the world did not recognize Him. He came to that which was His own, but His own did not receive Him. Yet to all who received Him, to those who believed in His name, He gave the right to become children of God" **(1:10–12)**.

Searching the Scriptures

1. What natural request did Mary and Martha's message to Jesus *not* contain **(11:3)**? See **Matthew 6:32**.

2. What did Jesus mean in **11:4** by "This sickness will not end in death"? Didn't Lazarus die?

3. We often refer to Jesus' death, resurrection, and ascension as His time of *glory*. For example in **7:39** we are told that the Spirit had not yet been given because Jesus was not yet *glorified*, which means that He had not yet died on the cross, rose again from the dead, and ascended into heaven. See also **12:16, 23**. With this special use of the words *glory* and *glorified* in John's gospel, what meanings do you think John wants us to find in **11:4**: "It is for God's *glory* so that God's Son may be *glorified* through it" (emphasis added)?

4. Jesus' response in **11:6** seems odd. We would expect Jesus to respond immediately. Why do you think He deliberately waited two days before going to Bethany? Might **2:1–11** and **7:1–10** give us a clue to a possible reason?

5. What euphemism did Jesus use in **11:11** to say that Lazarus was dead? See **Mark 5:39; Acts 7:60; 1 Corinthians 15:6; 1 Thessalonians 4:13.**

6. "I don't like crises," someone once said, "but I like the opportunities they supply." The death of Lazarus was a crisis, but Jesus also saw in it an opportunity **(11:15).** What did the disciples learn once again?

7. Why do you think John emphasized the length of time Lazarus had been in the tomb **(11:17, 39)**?

The three other gospels do not have the account of the raising of Lazarus. However, they all record the raising of Jairus' daughter **(Matthew 9:18–26; Mark 5:21–43; Luke 8:40–56)** and Luke also tells the story of the raising of the widow's son at Nain **(7:11–16).** An obvious difference between these occurrences and the one we are considering is the length of time that elapsed after the deaths. In the former, the restoration to life occurred shortly after the person had died; in the case of Lazarus, four days had elapsed.

8. Martha had once been rebuked by Jesus **(Luke 10:41)**, but she did not sulk at this time because of that. She rushed to meet Jesus while He was still on the road. When she met Him, what confidence did she express **(11:21–22)**? How do you understand our Lord's words in **11:25–26**? Martha's response to Jesus' statement that He is "the resurrection and the life" and that He gives immortality to those who believe in Him is a simple yet profound confession of faith **(11:27).** The last phrase, "who was to come into the world," is an expression used in Jesus' time to refer to the Messiah. See **1:9; 4:25; 6:14; Matthew 11:3.**

9. Mary greeted Jesus with the same words that Martha had used, but there is a difference: Mary "fell at His feet" **(11:32)**. This was the normal posture for showing great respect or worship. See **Mark 5:22; 10:17; Matthew 28:9.** Mary, who had once sat at Jesus' feet and listened to His teachings **(Luke 10:39),** now *fell* at His feet. What was Mary trying to say with her gesture?

10. Why did Jesus pray before raising Lazarus **(11:41–42)**?

11. The *Sanhedrin* **(11:47)** was the ruling council of the Jews. Many priests who were members of the Sanhedrin were also members of a sect called the Sadducees. Check whatever resources you have to find out about the Sadducees. Why were they particularly opposed to Jesus?

12. What was the concern expressed by the Sanhedrin **(11:47–48)**?

13. The high priest was supposed to be the spokesman of God to His people. He was looked to by the Jews as God's representative. That made his counsel **(11:49–50)** all the more diabolical and all the more ironic. What did Caiaphas mean? What was he recommending? In what far deeper sense were the words of Caiaphas true?

14. How does **11:52** help us interpret what Jesus said in **10:16**?

15. Why did Jesus leave Bethany and go to Ephraim near the wilderness **(11:54)**?

The Word for Us

1. Funeral customs vary drastically from country to country, and in our own land sometimes from one community to another. We seldom question or challenge the way things are done. At the time of a death decisions must be made quickly, and people are under extreme emotional strain. As Christians we want to do all things to the glory of God. Do the funeral practices that are accepted, perhaps even expected, in your community allow you to witness to the faith that you have as a Christian?

2. Nicodemus **(3:1–21)** was a member of the Sanhedrin. Can you imagine the conflict within his conscience if he was aware of the Sanhedrin plot to kill Jesus **(11:45–53)?** Should he challenge the high priest? Should he speak up for Jesus? Imagine that you are Nicodemus. What might you have done? Do you ever find yourself in the kind of situation he was in?

Closing

Read or sing together "I Am the Resurrection."

Refrain:

I am the Resurrection and the Life;
   They who believe in Me will never die.
I am the Resurrection and the Life;
   They who believe in Me will live a new life.

I have come to bring the truth;
I have come to bring you life;
If you believe, then you shall live.
Refrain

In My Word all people come to know
It is love which makes the spirit grow.
If you believe, then you shall live.
Refrain

Keep in mind the things that I have said;
Remember Me in the breaking of the bread.
If you believe, then you shall live.
Refrain

Lesson 9

The Final Trip to Jerusalem (John 12–13)

Theme Verse

"Hosanna! Blessed is He who comes in the name of the Lord! Blessed is the King of Israel!" **(John 12:13)**.

Goal

That Jesus never stopped loving, even as He walked down the road that led to His death. He remained faithful to His disciples even as they deserted Him.

What's Going On Here

After the raising of Lazarus Jesus was declared an outlaw. "The chief priests and Pharisees had given orders that if anyone found out where Jesus was, he should report it so that they might arrest Him" **(11:57)**. If we keep this fact in mind we will recognize Jesus' entry into Jerusalem for the incredibly courageous act that it was. He came boldly, openly, fully aware of the consequences. A throng of people came from Jerusalem to meet Him as He approached **(12:12–13)**. His riding into Jerusalem on a donkey was the fulfillment of prophecy **(Zechariah 9:9)**. But the crowd did not understand the significance of His actions, nor of what He said to the people later. This ended the public ministry of Jesus.

During an evening meal with the Twelve, Jesus gave them a lesson in humble service **(13:4–11)**. He reached out one last time to Judas, hoping to win his love and loyalty. When this attempt failed, Jesus told him to get on with the bloody scheme he thought was so secret. The disciples were not aware of the private drama being played out in their midst. Jesus told them that He was going away **(13:33)**. Peter asked to come along

(13:36–37). He claimed that nothing—not even death—would stop him. How little he realized of the enormity of Jesus' mission!

Searching the Scriptures
The Last Week (John 12)

1. The dinner at Bethany **(12:1–8)** was the last intimate social event that Jesus would enjoy with His friends. Four people were singled out by John for special comment: Martha, Lazarus, Mary, and Judas Iscariot. What do we learn about each of them from this episode?

2. Jesus' comment in **12:8** sounds as though He was unconcerned about the poor. What do you think He meant by His statement?

3. What was the significance of Jesus entering Jerusalem the way He did? (Hint: Remember that Jesus was the Messiah-King, but not the kind of messiah the people were expecting.)

4. John was a master in the use of irony and double entendre. **12:19** is a typical example. What were the Pharisees saying? What more profound truth were they also expressing, although without realizing it?

5. None of the other gospels include the incident in **12:20–22.** Why do you think John mentioned these Greeks who were seeking Jesus? To get a clue, go back to what immediately precedes this section.

6. In **12:24–26** Jesus speaks in the form of a paradox, that is, an assertion that is on the surface contradictory or opposed to common sense, but that is nevertheless true. Put these verses in your own words. What great truths was Jesus expressing?

7. John did not include the scene of Jesus struggling in the Garden of Gethsemane against the temptation to reject the path of suffering God set before Him. John does, however, describe Jesus fighting that battle in **12:27–33.** At what other crucial events in our Lord's life did the voice of God come to Him? See **Mark 1:11** and **9:7.**

8. Some interpret **12:32** to refer to the ascension and Jesus' return to power in heaven, but the context makes it clear that Jesus is talking about something else. What is it?

The term *Law,* used in **12:34,** is sometimes used to refer to the entire Old Testament. Some of the passages the people may have been thinking of are **Psalm 89:4; Isaiah 9:7; Ezekiel 37:25; Daniel 2:4; and 7:14.**
9. The meaning of **12:35–36** is clear in light of such passages as **John 1:9; 8:12; 9:4–5; 12:46.** What words in **12:36** indicate that Jesus is the light?

10. Did God make it impossible for some to believe in Jesus, as seems to be suggested in **12:39–40?**

11. John closes his record of Jesus' public ministry in **12:44–50.** In the chapters that follow Jesus would teach His disciples—not the people in general. These verses summarize and restate some of the dominant themes that we have encountered in the previous chapters. List or rephrase in your own words the main points of this final address of Jesus.

An Object Lesson in Humility (John 13)

1. Jesus' act of washing the feet of His disciples is all the more astounding when we consider the things He knew were to happen, the things that must have been going through His mind that evening **(13:1, 3).** What is so remarkable about His careful concern? What does His example mean for us? See also **Mark 10:35–45; Luke 22:24–27.**

2. Put **13:17** in your own words. Is knowing about Jesus' example of humility enough? See also **Luke 11:28.**

3. As in **13:19,** John emphasized many times the fact that Jesus knew what was going to happen to Him. John was insistent that nothing took Jesus by surprise or happened contrary to His intention. Why did Jesus tell His disciples what was going to happen in advance of the actual occurrence? Review your notes in this Study Guide on **6:20** and **8:58** for help on the expression "you will believe that *I am He*" in **13:19** (emphasis added).

4. *Before* Judas went out into the darkness of night **(13:30),** the *night* had entered into Him. When one leaves Jesus he leaves the Light. Apart from Him there is only darkness and death. In **13:31** Jesus declares that

the Son of Man is glorified. How did the departure of Judas lead to the glorification of Jesus?

5. Jesus urged His disciples to love one another as He had loved them (13:34). Think about the life of Jesus that you have been studying. How would you describe Jesus' love? What are some of its characteristics? How did He demonstrate His love for His disciples? Why is it so important that we who profess to be Christians demonstrate genuine love and unity that can be seen and recognized by people around us (13:35)?

The Word for Us

1. Read 12:42–43. Who were the secret disciples? It has been said that secret discipleship is a contradiction in terms, for either the secrecy kills the discipleship, or the discipleship kills the secrecy. Is it possible to be a secret disciple? When are you tempted to be a disciple in secret? How does the gospel of John encourage you to be a disciple in the open?

2. Jesus did not just *tell* us to love one another. He gave us a practical demonstration of how that love might look in action. The disciples probably never thought of washing each other's feet. That was for servants. What are some of the risks a disciple who washed the other disciples' feet would have taken? Can you share experiences in which your act of love exposed you to ridicule or to being taken advantage of? List and discuss ways in which you can take the risk that love requires and follow Jesus' example.

3. Jesus said, "Whoever serves Me must follow Me" **(12:26).** Think about our Lord's life. Into what sorts of situations did He go? With whom was He concerned? Try to translate His experience into today's setting. In very concrete, practical terms what do you think it means to *follow* Jesus today?

Closing

Read or sing "Draw Us to You."

Draw us to You,
And we will do
What You have taught forever
And hasten on
Where You have gone
To be with You, dear Savior.

Draw us to You
Each day anew.
Let us depart with gladness
That we may be
Forever free
From sorrow, grief, and sadness.

Draw us to You
That we stay true
And walk the road to heaven.
Direct our way
Lest we should stray
And from Your paths be driven.

Draw us to You;
Our hope renew;
Into Your kingdom take us.
Let us all there
Your glory share;
Your saints and joint heirs make us.

Lesson 10

When You Know You Are Going to Die (John 14–15)

Theme Verse

"Do not let your hearts be troubled. Trust in God; trust also in Me" (**John 14:1**).

Goal

In this session, we learn that Jesus spent His last day talking with His disciples, reassuring them and giving them guidance for the hard times ahead. We also find comfort and strength in His words.

What's Going On Here

Imagine, if you can, that you have only a few hours to live. You are strong and healthy. You do not want to die, but you are going to. You have one last chance to visit with those who are closest to you. What do you think you would talk about? It is hard to say, isn't it? But you probably would not waste your time on trivial or insignificant chatter. You would try to express what means most to you, what you would want to be remembered. You would probably tell people how you feel about them and what you hope for them.

In this and the next lesson we will be considering Jesus' last conversation with His disciples. He knew His time had come. What do you think was on His mind? What was so important to Him that He had to discuss it on that night? What did He talk about when He knew He was going to die?

Searching the Scriptures
Going Away to the Father (John 14)

1. The King James Version translates **14:2:** "In My Father's house are many mansions." The word *mansion* has a different meaning in English today than it did in the early 1600s when the King James Version was produced. It comes from the Latin word *mansio*, which means "a place to stay," "a lodging." The new translations correctly convey what Jesus was saying when they translate "In My Father's house are many *rooms.*" Jesus was not saying that heaven is made up of sumptuous palaces; rather He meant to say that in heaven there is room for all. Regardless of the translation, how do the words make you feel? What do they say about death? Your death?

2. If Jesus is "the way" **(14:6),** to what does He lead? See also **Ephesians 2:18** and **Hebrews 10:19–20.** Because Christianity is faith in Jesus, who called Himself "the way," check **Acts 9:2; 19:9;** and **22:4** to see what the Christian faith came to be called.

3. The core of Jesus' teaching is not the Sermon on the Mount. It is not a nobler and more demanding code of ethics. It is, rather, His claim to be absolutely, uniquely the Son of God. What related claims does He make in **14:6** and **14:10?**

4. What do you think Jesus meant when He said, "Anyone who has faith in Me will do what I have been doing. He will do even greater things than these, because I am going to the Father" **(14:12)?**

5. Does Jesus say in **14:13–14** that all our prayers, regardless of what

we pray for, will be granted? What does it mean to "ask in My name"?

6. Trying consistently to lead the Christian life, to keep the command-ments of Jesus (14:15, also 15:12), is a demanding task. Because Jesus knows we need help, what will He ask the Father to do (14:16)? Jesus is speaking about the Holy Spirit in 14:16–17. How does He refer to the Holy Spirit in these two verses? What do these expressions tell us about the function of the Holy Spirit?

7. What is it that the Holy Spirit does in the life of the believer (14:26)? What do you think Jesus meant when He said the Holy Spirit would "teach you *all things*" (emphasis added)?

Jesus was involved in much conflict; yet what did He offer as a parting gift to His followers (14:27)? See also **John 20:19, 21, 26; Romans 1:7; 5:1; Philippians 4:7; Colossians 3:15; 2 Thessalonians 3:16.**

The True Vine (John 15)

When Jesus spoke of Himself as "the true vine" (15:1) He was using a figure of speech well known to His disciples. The Old Testament common-ly refers to the nation of Israel under the form of a vine. (See **Psalm 80:8–16; Jeremiah 2:21; Ezekiel 19:10; Hosea 10:1;** and especially **Isa-iah 5:1–7.**) The Old Testament also represents Israel as a fig tree or an olive tree. It is of special significance that the imagery of the vine is only used in order to symbolize Israel's degeneration and to foretell her destruction.

1. What facts of spiritual life does Jesus express in **15:3?**

2. What does it mean to "remain in" Jesus **(15:4)?** How can we do that? Why is continual, personal contact with Jesus essential for us **(15:4–6)?**

3. It seems to say that Jesus has given us a blank check with which to draw on God's resources in **15:7.** How does the first part of the verse control effectively the second part? See the last part of **15:16** and **14:14.**

4. By leading productive, *fruit-bearing* lives we accomplish two things **(15:8).** What are they? See also **Matthew 5:14–16.**

5. What does **15:10** have to say about Christian obedience and Christian freedom?

6. People talk about "accepting Christ," "coming to Jesus," "taking the Lord into your life." What does **15:19** say about how we become a Christian? See also **Mark 3:13.**

The Word for Us

1. Jesus offers His peace to those who trust in Him. He tells them not to be afraid or troubled. Would you say, on the basis of these statements, that Christians are guaranteed a life free from anxiety, tension, uncertainty, and fear?

2. Jesus used the symbol of the vine and branches to describe the Christian's relationship to Himself. He said that the branches that bear fruit get pruned by God so they will bear even more fruit. Have you been conscious of this pruning in your life? If you have, what form has this pruning taken?

3. For many people their religion is a "gloomy" thing. They carry out their religious "duties" almost resentfully. What sort of things seem to take the joy out of your faith life? What experiences of faith have made you joyful? How is it possible to have joy even in times of sorrow? How would you compare joy with happiness or fun? Which is most important?

Closing

Read or sing together "What a Friend We Have in Jesus."

What a friend we have in Jesus,
All our sins and griefs to bear!
What a privilege to carry
Ev'rything to God in prayer!
Oh, what peace we often forfeit;
Oh, what needless pain we bear—
All because we do not carry
Ev'rything to God in prayer!

Have we trials and temptations?
Is there trouble anywhere?
We should never be discouraged—
Take it to the Lord in prayer.
Can we find a friend so faithful
Who will all our sorrows share?
Jesus knows our ev'ry weakness—
Take it to the Lord in prayer.

Are we weak and heavy-laden,
Cumbered with a load of care?
Precious Savior, still our refuge—
Take it to the Lord in prayer.
Do your friends despise, forsake you?
Take it to the Lord in prayer.
In His arms He'll take and shield you;
You will find a solace there.

Lesson 11

When You Know You Are Going to Die (Continued) (John 16–17)

Theme Verse

"All this I have told you so that you will not go astray" **(John 16:1)**.

Goal

That we learn the significance of how Jesus spent His last day before the crucifixion: in prayer for Himself, His disciples, and for us.

What's Going On Here

As we have seen, on the last night of His life Jesus was less concerned about what was going to happen to Him than what effect the events of the next few hours would have on His disciples. He tried to prepare them for the shattering experience of His capture, condemnation, and crucifixion. To do that Jesus turned for help to the same source to which He turned at all crucial events of His life, to His Father. **Chapter 17** is called the *High Priestly Prayer*. As High Priest Jesus consecrated Himself as the sacrifice that saves the world. The scope of the prayer widens as it progresses. Jesus started by praying for Himself. Then He prayed for His disciples who were with Him in the upper room. He ended by including in His prayer each of us along with the believers of all ages and places who were yet to come.

Searching the Scriptures
Prediction of Things to Come (John 16)

1. For Jesus the path to glory included rejection by people, exclusion from the synagogue **(Luke 4:28–29)**, and ultimately death—charged with blasphemy. Jesus wanted to prepare His followers for what inevitably comes to those who are loyal to Him. He offered, and still offers, a route to glory that goes by way of the cross. It is tragically true that the bitterest persecution often comes from those who think that by it they are serving God **(16:2)**. Can you think of an illustration of what Jesus predicted? Look up **Acts 26:9–11.**

2. We do not see events from God's perspective. Consequently, we sometimes imagine that we are suffering loss when we are actually experiencing great gain. We may think that things are working out to our detriment when God is actually accomplishing our good. An example of that is in **16:5–7.** Why was it to the disciples' advantage that Jesus leave them? A brief summary of the work of the Holy Spirit is given in **16:8–11.** It is very condensed and as a result may not be easy to understand. In what sense is the Spirit Christ's Spirit?

3. Whose righteousness is referred to in **16:10?** What does the second part of the verse have to do with the righteousness spoken of in the first part? See **Romans 3:21–26; Matthew 27:54; Luke 23:47; Acts 9:1–9.**

4. The last part of **16:11** helps us to understand the *judgment* referred to in the first part of this verse. See also **12:31** and **14:30.** What other judgment may also be meant?

5. What does Jesus promise that the Spirit will do for His disciples that He could not do at that time (16:12–13)? Do you think these verses apply to us as well as to the disciples to whom they were originally spoken? If you do, what do they tell us about our understanding of the significance of Jesus?

6. One of the functions of the Holy Spirit is to reveal what lies in the future (16:13). See also **Acts 2:17; Revelation 1:1; 22:6.** But what does **John 16:14** tell us is the main content of the Spirit's revelation to people? See **John 14:26** and **15:26.**

7. The disciples did not understand what Jesus meant in **16:16.** To what was He pointing?

8. According to **16:20,** what can Christians expect if they remain faithful to the Lord?

9. What does Jesus urge us to do in **16:24?** What does He want us to have? See also **15:11.**

10. Jesus makes a number of tremendous claims about Himself in **16:27–28.** He made the same claims in **3:13** and **13:3.** What does Jesus want to make sure His disciples understand about Himself?

The High Priestly Prayer (John 17)

1. What do you think of when you use the word *know?* Probably, we use *know* most often to express our intellectual grasp or understanding of factual information: "I know where he lives"; "Do you know what time it is?" Is that the way Jesus used the word *know* in **17:3?** What do we mean when we say, "She's a friend of mine. I *know* her well"?

2. When we give people gifts for their birthday or for Christmas we usually give them objects—a shirt, a CD, a pair of earrings. What gifts did God give His Son **(17:6)?** What gift does God give His church **(Ephesians 4:11)?** What is God's greatest gift to us?

3. Jesus said in **17:6,** "I have revealed Your *name* to those whom You gave Me" (emphasis added). The Jews did not separate the name of a person from the person himself. They thought of a person's name and his or her essential being as one. That is why Old Testament names were often statements describing people or places **(Genesis 17:5; 28:17–19; Exodus 3:14).** What other word could be substituted in the following passages for *name:* **Psalm 9:10; 20:7; 22:22; Isaiah 52:6?** What, then, is Jesus saying that He revealed?

4. On the basis of **17:9,** would it be correct to conclude that Jesus is concerned only with His disciples and not with the world? See **3:16; 4:42; 12:47.**

5. In **17:11–12** Jesus mentions God's name. Paraphrase these verses using what you learned in **17:6.**

6. Jesus is greatly concerned about the unity of His church. He prayed for it in **17:11** and again in **17:21–23.** When we see the loneliness and isolation that characterizes so many lives, the cruel hatred that separates classes, races, and nations, we can appreciate the need for unity for which our Lord prayed. Unity is a unique gift of God to the church. It also has a function in God's great plan to save the world. What is the oneness of Christ's followers designed to demonstrate?

7. The words of **17:15–18** need to be etched in our memories. The Christian faith is not so weak and delicate that it can survive only in cloistered seclusion from the world. Jesus does not want His followers to hide away in a monastery, a church, or a narrow, self-serving life. He has given us our marching orders. We are to follow Him. We are to go where He went. Where does He send us? For what does He pray as we live dangerously, daringly for Him?

Compare **17:17–18** with **10:36.** Jesus lived a sanctified life, and passed it on to His disciples. To *sanctify* (some translate the word as *consecrate*) means "to set apart for a special task." See God's appointment of Jeremiah **(Jeremiah 1:5)** and the establishment of the Old Testament priesthood **(Exodus 28:41).** This concept, associated with priestly service in the Old Testament, is also associated with Christ's sending His followers into the world. What does that tell us about the way He views ordinary life when it is lived to His glory? See **Romans 12:1–2.**

8. For whom is our Lord praying in **17:20–26?** Summarize what He prays for in this section.

The Word for Us

1. It has been said that unity is not merely a desirable feature of Christian existence; it is essential. Unity is not something that people can create, for God gives it; nor can people destroy it. What they can do, however, is obscure it. Discuss this theory of unity. Do you agree or disagree? Do the words of Jesus in **John 17:21–23** apply to the statement?

2. Sometimes the biblical accounts seem so distant and removed from our experience. In **17:20–26** we have not a story and not instruction, but Jesus praying for us. How does that feel? What difference might it make in our lives if we remember that we are not the only ones commanded to pray to God—but that Jesus and the Spirit are praying *for us?* What does that say about the importance and purpose of our life?

Closing

Read or sing together "Come, Holy Ghost, God and Lord."

Come, Holy Ghost, God and Lord,
With all Your graces now outpoured
On each believer's mind and heart;
Your fervent love to them impart.
Lord, by the brightness of Your light
In holy faith Your Church unite;
From ev'ry land and ev'ry tongue
This to Your praise, O Lord, our God, be sung:
Alleluia, alleluia!

Come, holy Light, guide divine,
Now cause the Word of life to shine.
Teach us to know our God aright
And call Him Father with delight.
From ev'ry error keep us free;
Let none but Christ our master be
That we in living faith abide,
In Him, our Lord, with all our might confide.
Alleluia, alleluia!

Come, holy Fire, comfort true,
Grant us the will Your work to do
And in Your service to abide;
Let trials turn us not aside.
Lord, by Your pow'r prepare each heart,
And to our weakness strength impart
That bravely here we may contend,
Through life and death to You, our Lord, ascend.
Alleluia, alleluia!

Lesson 12

The End and ...
(John 18–19)

Theme Verse

"For this reason I was born, and for this I came into the world, to testify to the truth" **(John 18:37)**.

Goal

That we learn that Jesus endured trials, persecutions, and even death in order to take away our sins.

What's Going On Here

Because we may be very familiar with the way Jesus died it is easy to miss much of what John was trying to tell us. Try to read these chapters as though you have never before heard the story of Jesus' death. As you read be alert to John's way of expressing his message in words that can have more than one meaning. Try to be sensitive to his use of symbolism and his allusions to the Old Testament. Especially remember that the crucifixion occurs at the time of the Passover. This is highly significant and symbolic in John's account of what takes place. Notice how John impresses on us that fact that what happens to Jesus happens with His foreknowledge. Though it looked to everyone as though His enemies were in complete control, the exact opposite was true. Pilate thought that he was trying Jesus, when in reality it was he that was on trial. Jesus was not forced to do anything against His will: He went to the cross of His own volition. He laid down His life; it was not taken from Him. When He knew that He had completed the work that His Father had given Him to do, He shouted out His victory and gave up His spirit. The end had come. It was all over. Or was it?

Searching the Scriptures

Jesus' Arrest and Appearance before the High Priest (John 18:1–27)

1. Judas led a large contingent of soldiers out to capture Jesus. They were evidently expecting that He would try to get away. Instead, what did He do **(18:4)**?

2. John has indicated previously that Jesus knew what was going to happen to Him—that He allowed it to happen. He was in control of events. How was this shown at the time of His capture? See also **Matthew 26:51–54.**

3. What is "the cup the Father has given Me" that Jesus says He must drink **(18:11)**? See **Mark 10:38; 14:36.**

The soldiers led Jesus to Annas **(18:13)**, who had been the high priest (A.D. 6–15), but had been deposed by the Romans. Four of his sons had also held the office of high priest. Caiaphas, who currently occupied the position, was his son-in-law. But Annas was clearly the power behind the throne and that is why Jesus was taken to him first.

4. Who was the other disciple spoken of in **18:15–16,** who followed and was known to the high priest?

5. Peter acted like a coward in the courtyard of the high priest. But that is only part of his story. He had also acted heroically. Which act that showed his loyalty to Jesus also put his life in danger?

Jesus before Pilate (John 18:28–19:16)

1. Notice how hatred had twisted the thinking of the Jews. They were intent on putting Jesus, an innocent man, to death, but what were they scrupulously careful to avoid **(18:28)**?

2. At first Pilate tried to avoid the responsibility of dealing with Jesus. He told the Jews to handle the case themselves **(18:31)**. If they had, they would have stoned Jesus for blasphemy **(Leviticus 24:16; John 8:59; 10:31; Acts 7:58)**. However, as a people subject to Rome they did not have the authority to execute anyone. It was necessary to get Jesus condemned under Roman law. Crucifixion was the Roman method of execution. Even in this maneuver the Jews were unwitting participants in the fulfillment of a prophecy made by Jesus **(18:32)**. See **3:14; 8:28; 12:32–33**. With what did they accuse Jesus before Pilate **(18:33–35)**?

3. In response to Pilate's question, "Are You the king of the Jews?" Jesus answered, "Is that your own idea ... or did others talk to you about Me?" What did Jesus mean by that response? Why didn't He answer simply and directly: "Yes, I am the king of the Jews"?

4. Do you see irony in Pilate's question in **18:38?** What is the answer to what he is asking? See **1:14, 17; 8:31–32; 14:6**.

5. Why did Pilate have Jesus flogged if he believed that He was not guilty of any crime?

6. What was the real reason for the Jews' hatred of Jesus **(19:7)**?

7. Why do you think Jesus refused to answer Pilate **(19:9)**?

8. The Jews could see that Pilate was sympathetic toward Jesus and wanted to let Him go. What tactic did they resort to, to get Pilate to condemn Jesus **(19:12)**?

9. In **19:14** John noted that it was "the day of Preparation of Passover Week." The eating of a lamb was part of the Passover celebration. What was done to the Passover lambs on the day of preparation? How is that significant of what John wrote about?

10. Read again John's prolog **(1:1–18)**. Of what prolog verse does the entire episode before Pilate remind you, especially the final answer of the chief priests: "We have no king but Caesar"?

Jesus' Crucifixion and Burial (John 19:17–42)

1. The inscription that Pilate placed on Jesus' cross **(19:19)** was undoubtedly phrased to irritate the Jews. Pilate was totally unconscious of the deeper sense in which the words were true. Why do you think John mentioned that the charge nailed to the cross was written in Aramaic

(Hebrew), Latin, and Greek **(19:20)?**

The linen tunic worn by the high priest was traditionally one piece of cloth, woven without a seam. By drawing attention to the fact that Jesus' tunic was identical to that of the high priest, John may have been making a comment not simply about what Jesus wore but about who He was **(19:23)**. See **Hebrews 2:17** and **4:14–5:5**.

2. To give Jesus some relief from His thirst, a sponge was soaked in wine vinegar and then put on a stalk of *hyssop* **(19:29)**. We have seen how John tried to tie in Christ's crucifixion to the Passover that the Jews were about to celebrate. See **Exodus 12:22** for the use of *hyssop* in the Passover. What connection does John want us to make?

3. John recorded the last words spoken by Jesus on the cross **(19:30)**. **Matthew 27:50** and **Mark 15:37** tell us how He uttered these words. What was Jesus referring to when He said, "It is finished?"

4. The fact that, in contrast to the two thieves with whom He was crucified, the legs of Jesus were not broken is highly significant to anyone familiar with Passover regulations. See **Exodus 12:46; Numbers 9:12; 1 Corinthians 5:7**. There also seems to be profound symbolism in **19:32–37**. Of what do the water and the blood that flowed from the pierced side of Jesus remind you? See **4:14; 6:53–57; 7:37–39; 1 John 1:7; 5:6–8**.

The Word for Us

1. Select one of the principal characters in this portion of Scripture

(Pilate, Peter, Jesus, John, the high priest, Mary, etc.). Try to get into the experience of that person. What did the events of these chapters mean to him/her? How did he/she feel? Why did the person act the way he/she did? What strengths or weaknesses are evident? What did he/she think the day after the crucifixion? How are you like that character? Is that a gift of God or is it a personal weakness? What does the event of the crucifixion mean to you?

2. The crucifixion is part of the *light*. It exposes our needs, our weaknesses, and our sins, while at the same time it reveals the act of God that forgives and saves us. What message is most clear to you in the crucifixion: the Law, which condemns, or the Gospel, which saves? What portion of these chapters is most important to you? Why?

Closing

Read or sing together "O Sacred Head, Now Wounded."

O sacred head, now wounded,
    With grief and shame weighed down,
Now scornfully surrounded
    With thorns, Your only crown.
O sacred head, what glory
    And bliss did once combine;
Though now despised and gory,
    I joy to call You mine!

How pale You are with anguish,
    With sore abuse and scorn!
Your face, Your eyes now languish,
    Which once were bright as morn.
Now from Your cheeks has vanished
    Their color once so fair;
From loving lips is banished
    The splendor that was there.

All this for my transgression,
  My wayward soul to win;
This torment of Your Passion,
  To set me free from sin.
I cast myself before You,
  Your wrath my rightful lot;
Have mercy, I implore You,
  O Lord, condemn me not!

Here will I stand beside You,
  Your death for me my plea;
Let all the world deride You,
  I clasp You close to Me.
My awe cannot be spoken,
  To see You crucified;
But in Your body broken,
  Redeemed, I safely hide!

What language can I borrow
  To thank You, dearest friend,
For this Your dying sorrow,
  Your mercy without end?
Bind me to You forever,
  Give courage from above;
Let not my weakness sever
  Your bond of lasting love.

Lord, be my consolation,
  My constant source of cheer;
Remind me of Your Passion,
  My shield when death is near.
I look in faith, believing
  That You have died for me;
Your cross and crown receiving,
  I live eternally.

Lesson 13

... the Beginning
(John 20–21)

Theme Verse

"These [things] are written that you may believe that Jesus is the Christ, the Son of God, and that believing you may have life in His name" **(John 20:31)**.

Goal

In this session, we learn that the end of Jesus was not the end. He died on the cross, but after three days He rose from the dead so that we too may rise again to everlasting life.

What's Going On Here

When Jesus' enemies nailed Him to the cross, they wiped their hands and said to themselves, "Well, that takes care of Him. We won't be seeing Him anymore." Nor were they the only ones who thought that. For Jesus' disciples, Good Friday seemed to be the end of their world, the dissolution of all their hopes. Although Jesus had tried to prepare them for what He knew was going to take place, they did not grasp the significance of what He had told them. They were too much the products of their age. They could not believe that messiahship involved suffering and death. They did not expect the crucifixion and, as a result, they were not ready for the resurrection.

John wants us to know that the resurrection was as astounding to the original followers of Jesus as it is to us. But he also wants us to be sure that it actually occurred. Not only did Jesus rise from the dead but He appeared to various people on more than one occasion. The resurrection is pivotal to the Christian proclamation. Paul put it as concisely as anyone could want it: "If Christ has not been raised, our preaching is useless and so is your faith. More than that, we are then found to be false witnesses about God, for we have testified about God that He raised Christ from the dead. ... But Christ has indeed been raised from the dead, the firstfruits of those who have fallen asleep. ... Thanks be to God! He gives us the victory through our Lord Jesus Christ" (1 Corinthians 15:14–15, 20, 57). His enemies thought they had put an end to Jesus. The cross was just the beginning.

Searching the Scriptures
The Resurrection (John 20)

All of the gospels concur that it was not the male disciples who went to the tomb first on Easter Sunday morning, but the women followers of Jesus (Matthew 28:1; Mark 16:1–3; Luke 23:55–24:2). As they had remained to witness His crucifixion (19:25) so it is fitting that they should be the first to witness His resurrection.

1. According to 20:2, who was still recognized as the leader of the disciples?

2. Mary Magdalene went to the tomb to mourn the death of Jesus and to anoint His body with spices (Mark 16:1). She was not expecting what she found. As a result what did she conclude (20:2)?

3. Why do you think John notes (20:6–7) the precise condition and position of the cloths that had been wrapped around the body of Jesus?

4. How do you interpret 20:9?

5. As happened so often before His crucifixion, so also now after His resurrection Jesus was not immediately recognized **(20:14)**. Why did Mary mistake Jesus' true identity?

6. When Mary realized that the person she was talking to was not the gardener but Jesus, what did she do **(20:17)?** See **Matthew 28:9.**

7. We have seen how simple and direct witnessing about Jesus can be **(1:41, 45; 4:29; 9:25).** How did Mary go about witnessing about the risen Lord **(20:18)?** How can you apply this simple style of witnessing to your life?

8. Jesus' actions in **20:21–23** have been referred to as the institution of the Christian church. According to **20:21,** what does Jesus commission His church to do? See also **17:18; Matthew 28:19–20; Acts 1:8.**

9. Does the first part of **20:22** bring to mind any verse of the Old Testament? Can you recall another time when God *breathed* and something special happened? See **Genesis 2:7.** Jesus had said that He would send His Spirit to the disciples **(14:16, 26; 15:26; 16:7).** Here He fulfills that promise.

10. What great privilege and authority did Jesus give to His disciples (**20:23**)?

11. Thomas was so crushed by the events of Good Friday that he had withdrawn from the company of the other disciples. Whom else had he isolated himself from (**20:24**)? When Jesus appeared to the disciples a week after Easter, He singled out Thomas for special attention. Try to put yourself in Jesus' position. What do you think you might have said to Thomas?

12. John wanted everyone to know that what he recorded was true. He and the other disciples were eyewitnesses to what he related (**1:14; 1 John 1:1–3**). That is important. But not everyone could be alive when Jesus lived among people on earth. Not everyone could see Him as Thomas and the others did. Does that put us at a disadvantage or make us somehow less favored? Consider the words of our Lord in **20:29** and **17:20**.

13. John wrote that his gospel was not intended to be a biography or a complete account of Jesus' life. He was selective in what he included in his gospel. What was his controlling interest and ultimate purpose in writing? See **John 20:30–31** and **21:25**.

The Risen Lord Shows Himself (John 21)

The episode related in the first half of **chapter 21** recalls a similar incident recorded in **Luke 5:1–11**. Compare that incident to this one.

1. Who was the first one to recognize that the man on the shore was the Lord **(21:7)?** Who was the first one to act?

2. Notice the different reaction by Peter on this occasion in comparison to the similar occurrence recorded in **Luke 5:1–11.** What had changed? Was Peter no longer conscious of being a sinner?

3. We have seen that John—and the same is true for the other gospel writers—did not insert details unless they were significant. What do you think is the significance of his mentioning the precise number of fish caught by the disciples and the fact that "even with so many the net was not torn" **(21:11)?**

4. Three times Jesus ask Peter the same question. Would not once have been enough? What is the point of the repetition? See **13:37–38; Mark 14:27–31; John 18:17, 25, 27.** What did Jesus mean when He said to Peter: "Feed My lambs ... take care of My sheep ... feed my sheep"?

5. Considering **21:18,** what do you think the expression *you will stretch out your hands* means?

John ends his gospel with the tantalizing reminder that he recorded only a small part of all the things that Jesus did. But even if we had a complete account of all that He had done and said we would still never be able adequately to explore or express the inexhaustible significance of what it means that "the Word became flesh and made His dwelling among us … full of grace and truth" (1:14).

The Word for Us

1. If you did not begin the lesson with a discussion of Jesus' encounters with Mary, Thomas, and Peter (see the Leaders Notes) do so now, or continue your discussion. Each of the three people mentioned was suffering from a common human need:

a. Mary was grieving (20:11–18). How did she feel? Have you ever felt grief like that? How did Jesus deal with Mary's grief? How does this encounter give you hope in your grief?

b. Thomas doubted (20:26–29). How did he feel? How are disappointment, depression, and doubt often connected? When have you doubted and felt far from God? How did Jesus deal with Thomas' doubt? How does the message of these chapters give you confidence in the face of your doubts?

c. Peter was guilty. He had denied his Lord. How did he feel when Jesus started to question him about his loyalty (21:15–19)? Have you ever felt guilty like that? How did Jesus deal with Peter's guilt? How does the message of the resurrection of Jesus give you a way to overcome your guilt when it threatens your peace of mind? Through whom does the message of forgiveness come?

2. Discuss some of the ways in which you might become a "messenger" of the risen Lord that the people of these chapters became. What joyful Word do we share? In what sense are we involved in our eternal life right now? What qualifies us to be messengers for Christ?

Closing

Sing or read together "He's Risen, He's Risen."

He's risen, He's risen, Christ Jesus, the Lord;
Death's prison He opened, incarnate, true Word.
Break forth, hosts of heaven, in jubilant song
While earth, sea, and mountain the praises prolong.

The foe was triumphant when on Calvary
The Lord of creation was nailed to the tree.
In Satan's domain his hosts shouted and jeered,
For Jesus was slain, whom the evil ones feared.

But short was their triumph, the Savior arose,
And death, hell, and Satan He vanquished, His foes;
The conquering Lord lifts His banner on high.
He lives, yes, He lives, and will nevermore die.

Oh, where is your sting, death? We fear you no more;
Christ rose, and now open is fair Eden's door.
For all our transgressions His blood does atone;
Redeemed and forgiven, we now are His own.

Then sing your hosannas and raise your glad voice;
Proclaim the blest tidings that all may rejoice.
Laud, honor, and praise to the Lamb that was slain;
In glory He reigns, yes, and ever shall reign.

JOHN
The Word Became Flesh

Leaders Notes

Preparing to Teach John

It is frustrating to try to condense the gospel of John into a course of 13 lessons. There is such a marvelous abundance of material that one could never talk about or react to all of it. This study is designed to alert the student to some of the insights that await his or her more careful reading—a lifelong reading. This study will have served one of its purposes if it whets the student's appetite to return to John's gospel after this class is over.

In preparation to teach, read through the entire book of John, preferably in a modern translation. The NIV is generally referred to in the lesson comments of this guide. Get in tune with John's rhythm and style of writing. Also consult writings about the book of John, such as the introduction to John in the *Concordia Self-Study Bible*. If possible, read the section on John in the *Concordia Self-Study Commentary*. The following commentaries are useful resources for the study of John: *The Gospel according to John*, by Leon Morris (Eerdmans, 1971); *The Gospel of John*, by F. F. Bruce (Eerdmans, 1983).

If you have any questions about what you read, write them down, then consult a commentary or your pastor for answers. Make notations in your Bible, in this guide, or in a separate notebook about any insights you learn in your study. Share these with the class participants if time allows.

In the section "Searching the Scriptures," the leader serves as a guide, using the questions given (or others) to help the class discover what the text actually says. This is a major part of teaching, namely, directing the learners to discover for themselves. Another major portion of each lesson is helping the students through discussion to see the meaning for our times, for church and world today, and especially for our own lives.

Group Bible Study

Group Bible study means mutual learning from one another under the guidance of a leader or facilitator. The Bible is an inexhaustible resource. No one person can discover all it has to offer. In a class many eyes see many things and can apply them to many life situations. The leader should resist the temptation to "give the answers" and to act as an "authority." This teaching approach stifles participation by individual members and can actually hamper learning. As a general rule the teacher is not to "give interpretation" but to "develop interpreters." Of course, there are times when the leader should and must share insights and information gained by his or her own deeper research. The ideal class is one in which the leader guides class members through the lesson and engages them in meaningful sharing and discussion at all points, leading them to a summary of the lesson at the close. As a general rule, don't tell what the learners can discover by themselves.

The general aim of every Bible study is to help people grow spiritually, not merely in biblical and theological knowledge, but also in Christian thinking and living. This means growth in Christian attitudes, insights, and skills for Christian living. The focus of this course must be the church and the world of our day. The guiding question will be, What does the Lord teach us for life today through the book of John?

Pace Your Teaching

Do not try to cover every question in each lesson. This would lead to undue haste and frustration. Be selective. Pace your teaching. Spend no more than five minutes with the "Theme Verse" and "Goal" and two or three minutes with "What's Going On Here." Allow 20 minutes to apply the lesson ("The Word for Us") and five minutes for "Closing." This schedule, you will notice, allows only about 30 minutes for working with the text ("Searching the Scriptures").

Should your group have more than a one-hour class period, you can take it more leisurely. But do not allow any lesson to drag and become tiresome. Keep it moving. Keep it alive. Keep it deeply meaningful. Eliminate some questions and restrict yourself to those questions most meaningful to the members of the class. If most members study the text at home, they can report their findings, and the time gained can be applied to relating the lesson to life.

Good Preparation

Good preparation by the leader usually affects the pleasure and satisfaction the class will experience.

Suggestions to the Leader for Using the Study Guide

The Lesson Pattern

The material in this guide is designed to aid *Bible study*, that is, a consideration of the written Word of God, with discussion and personal application growing out of the text at hand. The typical lesson is divided into these sections:

1. Theme Verse
2. Goal
3. What's Going On Here
4. Searching the Scriptures
5. The Word for Us
6. Closing

"Theme Verse" and "Goal" give the leader assistance in arousing the interest of the group in the concepts of the lesson. In these notes for you, the leader, these two sections are covered under "Getting Started" because that is their purpose: to get the learners to start thinking about the lesson. Do not linger too long over the introductory remarks. Use them merely to show that the material to be studied is meaningful to Christian faith and life today.

"What's Going On Here" helps you gain an understanding of the textual portion to be considered in the session. Before the text is broken down for closer scrutiny, it should be seen in the perspective of a greater whole. At this point the class leader takes the participants to a higher elevation to show them the general layout of the lesson. The overview gives the group an idea where it is going, what individual places are to be visited, and how the two are interrelated.

"Searching the Scriptures" provides the real "spadework" necessary for Bible study. Here the class digs, uncovers, and discovers; it gets the facts and observes them. Comment from the leader is needed only to the extent that it helps the group understand the text. The questions in the Study Guide are intended to help the learners discover the meaning of the text.

Having determined what the text says, the class is ready to apply the message. Having heard, read, marked, and learned the Word of God, we proceed to digest it inwardly through discussion, evaluation, and application. This is done, as the Study Guide suggests, by taking the truths of John and applying them to the world and Christianity in general and then to personal Christian life. Class time may not permit discussion of all the questions and topics.

Remember, the Word of God is sacred, but the Study Guide is not. The guide offers only suggestions. The leader should not hesitate to alter the guidelines or substitute others to meet his or her needs and the needs of the participants. Adapt your teaching plan to your class and your class period. Good teaching directs the learner to discover for himself or herself. For the teacher this means directing the learner, not giving the learner answers. Choose the verses that should be looked up in Scripture. What discussion questions will you ask? At what points? Write them in the margin of your Study Guide. Involve class members, but give them clear directions.

Begin the class time with prayer, and allow time for a brief time of worship at the end of the class session. Suggestions for brief closing devotions are given in the Study Guide. Remember to pray frequently outside of class for yourself and your class. May God the Holy Spirit bless your study and your leading of others into the comforting truths of God's Christ-centered Word.

Lesson 1
In the Beginning (John 1)

Before the Session

Before your first session, carefully read through the first chapter of John. Get to your classroom or teaching area early to make sure chairs and tables are set up, lighting is adequate, and the air temperature is comfortable. Have extra Bibles, pens or pencils, and paper available for participants.

Getting Started

Class members will feel much more comfortable and be more willing to share if they know the other participants. Especially at the start of this first session, give the participants time to talk to one another. You may wish to have members talk to each other in pairs, then have them introduce their partner. After the introductions, pray that Jesus, the Word become flesh, will guide you and your class members as you study His Word in this session. Then begin by having volunteers read the "Theme Verse" and "Goal."

What's Going On Here

Ask a volunteer to read the paragraphs under this heading in the Study Guide. They will provide an introduction to the book of John and to the course. If time permits and you believe your class would be interested, share all or some of the following additional background:

The author of the fourth gospel was John, "the beloved disciple," the brother of James, who along with his brother and with Peter, was present during some of the most important moments of our Lord's earthly ministry **(Mark 9:2; 14:33).** Tradition states that the apostle John spent much of his later life in Ephesus, a city in western Asia Minor. John lived to be a very old man. Consequently, Ephesus is usually considered the place where the gospel was written, perhaps around A.D. 85. It is interesting to note that one of the oldest portions of the New Testament that we possess is a papyrus fragment of a manuscript of the gospel of John. This fragment contains only **John 18:31–33** and **37–38,** but it has helped to establish that the gospel was written much earlier than many scholars once believed.

Clement of Alexandria, who died around A.D. 220, is quoted by the ancient historian Eusebius as saying: "Last of all, John, perceiving that what had reference to the bodily things of Jesus' ministry had been sufficiently related, and encouraged by his friends, and inspired by the Holy Spirit, wrote a spiritual gospel" (*The Church History of Eusebius*, book 6, chapter 14, number 7). He meant that John took a different approach from the other writers who had given the details of the life of Christ. John was interested in showing who this Jesus of Nazareth is and the meaning of His life for the world. Thus John started his gospel with a prolog: **John 1:1–18** is a short but profound theological essay on who Jesus is.

Jesus is true God, who existed before the world came into being. He participated in the world's formation. He ultimately became a human being and lived in the world He had created. He was so much a human being that most of His contemporaries refused to believe that He was anything more. Yet He was also fully God. A few, His disciples, perceived the glory of God in Jesus as it was shown in the truth He expressed and the loving way He dealt with people.

Searching the Scriptures

The Prolog (John 1:1–18)

1. In order to emphasize Jesus' connection with creation and life, John began his gospel with the very same words that begin the creation account in Genesis.

2. In **1:1–4** John says that Jesus, the Word of God, was present at the beginning of things. He was *with* God, in intimate association with Him. More than that, Jesus *was* God. The entire world came into existence through Him. He not only contains life; He *is* life.

3. The Old Testament passages indicate that God's Word is eternal and powerful. When God created "in the beginning," He created by means of His Word. Without fail, God's Word accomplishes His purposes. The Word gave life to creation. This same life-giving Word of God became flesh in the person of Jesus Christ, who is God. He is a person of the Trinity, the one God in three persons: Father, Son, and Holy Spirit. See also **Hebrews 1:1–3.**

4. Although misunderstood by many, the light of the world will never be overcome by the darkness of sin, Satan, and death.

5. The greatness of John the Baptizer lay in his recognition of his unimportance compared to Jesus. John did not want people to become attached to him as a preacher. He wanted them to accept his proclamation that Jesus was the Messiah. John testified that Jesus had surpassed him because He was before him. John had come to point people to the Messiah. That was his mission. Jesus, on the other hand, was the Messiah. John was the poster that advertised a coming attraction. Jesus was the event itself.

6. Only those who through God's grace have received Jesus, who

believe in His name, have been given the right by God to become His children.

7. As God had dwelt among His people in the tabernacle, so He had now come to dwell among His people in the Word made flesh. The glory of God that was seen in the cloud in the Old Testament was now seen in the living Word. And that Word exhibited the characteristics of grace and truth so prominently proclaimed about God in the Old Testament.

8. Moses was like Jesus in that he was specially chosen by God. Like Jesus he was the mediator or "middleman" between God and His people. He was called by God to lead His people out of captivity. On a mountain (Sinai) God revealed His will for His people to Moses. And after Moses spoke with God on the mountain, his face was so radiant with the glory of God that the people were afraid to come near him. Yet for all their similarities Moses was only a human being. The captivity out of which he led the people of God was physical enslavement. On a mountain (Calvary) God revealed His plan of forgiveness for His people. Jesus is both God and man. He is the unique mediator of God to people and of people to God. He frees people from spiritual enslavement to sin, death, and Satan. The will of God that Moses proclaimed was the Law, summarized in the Ten Commandments. Jesus brought grace and truth and made known the Father. From the fullness of Jesus' grace we receive what the Law could not give us because of our sin—forgiveness, life, and salvation.

The Witness of John the Baptizer (John 1:19–34)

1. Jesus was foreshadowed in Abraham's willingness to offer Isaac as a sacrifice and particularly in the lamb that God dramatically provided to take Isaac's place (Genesis 22). The lamb was central to the annual celebration of the Passover (Exodus 12). Jesus is our Passover Lamb. He is the Suffering Servant whom Isaiah described going to His death as a lamb goes to slaughter. Yet this lamb, seemingly so weak and helpless, brought victory by His death. He won the bitter battle with death. Therefore the book of Revelation pictures Jesus, the Lamb of God, as conqueror.

2. The baptism of John was a sign and expression of the repentance of the person baptized. The baptism of Jesus, in contrast, confers God's Holy Spirit on the receiver. Jesus still gives His Spirit to the church through Baptism today. John would have us see that it is not really we who baptize; it is the risen Lord who is mightily at work in the Sacrament of Baptism whenever and wherever it is performed in His name.

The First Disciples (John 1:35–51)

1. After spending the day listening to Jesus preach, Andrew was convinced that He was the Messiah. The Word continues to have power today.

The Holy Spirit works through God's Word to create and to strengthen saving faith in Jesus.

2. Philip and Andrew's "strategy" was simply to tell others the "message" that Jesus is the Messiah. We often have the idea that witnessing means answering questions about Christianity or "talking religion." We may be uncomfortable with that kind of witnessing because we do not consider ourselves to be fluent speakers or to be trained in theology. But what Andrew and Philip did was really very simple. They invited people to meet Jesus. They did not try to prove anything. They did not attempt to argue or defend their position. They only invited others to experience Jesus for themselves. Jesus had convinced them that He was the Christ. Jesus had invited them to come and see. And that is what Andrew and Philip invited Peter and Nathanael to do. They had spent some time with Jesus. That made the difference. Before we can witness for Jesus we must know Him ourselves.

The Word for Us

The thrust of the opening portion of John's gospel is his emphasis on the involvement of God in the world and in our lives. The four questions will help you and the class think about some of the ways in which the truth of Christ's presence in the world and in us becomes real for us.

1. Answers will vary.

2. That God the Son became a flesh-and-blood person affirms the goodness of God's creation of the body as well as the soul (see **Genesis 1:26–27, 31**). God declared the entirety of His creation good. The problem with people—soul and body—is that they have been corrupted by sin; not that their soul is imprisoned in their body.

3. Answers will vary.

4. Emphasize that witnessing is not always a program or a system. It is as well our simple affirmation of our faith in Christ and the direct invitation to those about us to come and see.

Closing

Follow the suggestion in the Study Guide. If you feel comfortable doing so, lead the class in prayer, asking the Holy Spirit to give you and the participants of this study the courage to tell others that Jesus is the Christ, just as Andrew and Philip did.

Lesson 2
Miraculous Signs (John 2)

Before the Session

Carefully read through **John 2.** Again, get to your teaching area early to check the comfort level and the availability of Bibles.

Getting Started

Renew the introductions from last session. Pray, asking the God of miracles to renew the miracles of faith and understanding in your hearts as you study today. Then begin by having volunteers read the "Theme Verse" and "Goal."

What's Going On Here

Ask a member of the class to read the two paragraphs under this heading in the Study Guide. It will serve as an introduction to the study of the chapter.

As time permits, share the following information about the term *miraculous sign*, which John used several times in this chapter when speaking of the works performed by Jesus.

John says that the changing of water into wine was "the first of His *miraculous signs*" (**2:11, emphasis added**). Because of Jesus' disruption of the business activity going on in the temple, the Jews demanded: "What *miraculous sign* can You show us to prove Your authority to do all this?" (**2:18, emphasis added**). The New Testament uses three different words in referring to the miracles of Jesus. It uses *teras*, which means "anything that causes wonder or astonishment." It uses *dunamis*, which means "power or might." And it uses *semeion*, which means "sign." *Semeion* is the favorite word of John and is very instructive. It points us in the direction we must look if we want to understand the basic purpose of Jesus' miracles. John wants us to realize that Jesus did not perform miracles in order to astound people, to overwhelm them and thereby force them to believe in Him. God does not strong-arm anyone into faith. The miracles that Jesus performed did not prove to everyone who saw them that He was the Messiah. They usually produced wonder, but not faith. But they were not tricks—they were *miraculous signs*—and only a few people read those signs correctly. Jesus' miracles, such as the one at Cana, were intended to convey a message. They were done to declare who Jesus was and through Him to reveal God Himself. The people missed the point. They demanded signs for proof. The signs spoke clearly. They did not understand. They could not understand. They lacked faith in Jesus. We are still often confused about miracles. We think that signs (miracles) make Jesus believable. They do not. It is faith that makes the signs meaningful and understandable.

Searching the Scriptures

The Wedding at Cana (John 2:1–11)

1. Jesus was concerned about ordinary people who lived their lives in humble circumstances. He went to the small villages and towns, such as Cana. He did not reserve Himself for the big crowds in important metropolitan centers. He came for all. He didn't just speak in the temple, but went out to where the people were—even to weddings. His Gospel was not reserved for the rich, beautiful, and famous; but also for the poor, handicapped, and common **(Luke 7:22)**.

2. Jesus addressed His mother with the words *dear woman* when He hung on the cross **(John 19:26)**; obviously He was very concerned about her at the time. Jesus' answer to His mother might better be expressed: "Don't worry; you don't understand what is going on; but I'll handle things in my own way." Jesus knew the importance of doing things at the right time. Even His death occurred at the right time to save the world.

3. Jesus is the "new wine" referred to in **Mark 2:22.** The people who questioned His style of life—it was not "religious" enough—were told that just as new wine must have new containers to hold it, so the joy and exhilaration He brings cannot be compressed and expressed in the old forms of fasting and conventional religious piety.

The Cleansing of the Temple (John 2:12–25)

1. The money changers and sellers of animals provided a valid and helpful service to those who came to worship in Jerusalem. Our Lord did not become angry because of *what* they were doing but because of *the way* and *the place* in which they were doing it. He could not abide the way they fleeced the poor and dispossessed the Gentiles of their rightful place of worship.

2. Jesus was angered for the following reasons:

a. The pilgrims who came to the temple from all over Palestine and the countries beyond could not make their offerings with their local currency. They had to exchange it for special money used in the temple. The priests authorized money changers to provide this service in the temple area. However, these money changers, with the priests' permission, gouged the pilgrims by charging them exorbitant rates for the service they provided.

b. The sellers of sacrificial animals demanded outlandish prices for their animals, 10 and 20 times what they could be bought for elsewhere. Even if a person brought his or her own animal from home or purchased it in the city marketplace, the temple inspectors, appointed by the priests, invariably rejected it as being imperfect. Thus the worshipers, particularly the poor, were being taken advantage of—and all in the name of religion.

c. All of this business activity was going on right in the temple, in the Court of the Gentiles. This was the only place in the temple that was open to Gentiles for prayer. With all the bartering, animal noises, and general confusion, what chance did a Gentile have to find a quiet place conducive to worship? It was apparently because of the inconsideration being shown to the Gentile worshipers that our Lord became angry.

3. Jesus certainly did not threaten to tear down the temple, as the Jews thought. He did predict its destruction **(Mark 13:2).** He may very well have said that the temple had fulfilled its purpose in God's plan. But as John states **(2:21),** our Lord's contemporaries misunderstood His statement about the destruction of the temple in **2:19.** He was not making a threat to a building but a prediction about Himself.

The Word for Us

These discussion questions lead us to look at the example of Jesus as it is revealed in this portion of the Gospel. What does the way He lived and acted say to us about our lives now? The purpose of these questions is not to simply find fault with ourselves and others, but to recognize the way in which the perfect obedience of Jesus exposes our weaknesses and our need to ask for His forgiveness in our lives.

1. We often find it easier to love from a distance. Sometimes it is hard to love the people we see around us every day. To them, we often express more criticism than love. When we find ourselves being critical and not loving, then we can repent of those sins and ask God to forgive us through Christ. Only then can the love we have been shown in Christ show through us to those we love.

2. Sometimes Christianity is somber. Sometimes we lean harder on the "don'ts" in our religious practice than the "dos." How does a Christian express joy? Try to help the class catch some of the flavor of happiness that Jesus seems to indicate is a part of our celebration of life.

3. Anger itself is not sinful. God becomes angry. But anger can be destructive, especially if it is saved or misdirected. Talk about some ways to deal with anger. Anger is a terrible burden for some. Help those who need to share their hurt. Encourage them to take the burden of their anger to Christ for forgiveness and to ask His power to overcome their anger.

Closing

Follow the suggestion in the Study Guide. If you feel comfortable doing so, lead the class in prayer, asking God for His continued blessing on you and your participants as you go forth to live out His miracle of love in your everyday lives.

Lesson 3

Two Who Misunderstood (John 3:1–4:42)

Before the Session

Read carefully through **John 3:1–4:42,** jotting down any notes and questions. Arrive early in your teaching area. Is it warm enough? cool enough? light enough? Are the chairs and tables set up? Make sure there are enough Bibles and pens or pencils.

Getting Started

Introduce any new participants who may be joining you. Begin with a prayer, asking Jesus to keep your hearts and minds clear of misunderstandings as you study His Word. Then have volunteers read the "Theme Verse" and "Goal."

What's Going On Here

The paragraphs under this heading in the Study Guide again serve as an introduction to the readings. You may read them aloud or summarize them in your own words. You may wish to refer to the following background information on the Pharisees in your discussion of Nicodemus:

The Interview with Nicodemus (John 3:1–21)

Nicodemus was a Pharisee, one of the few who were not hostile toward Jesus. In general, the Pharisees were Jesus' most vigorous antagonists. They resented Him because He had the authority they craved and would not share it with them. His style of life was contrary to everything that they considered religious. The Pharisees were a brotherhood who devoted their lives to keeping all the regulations of the Jewish religious law. Pharisees had no time for anything other than the law. They separated themselves from ordinary pursuits. Even the name *Pharisee* means "separate." For the

Pharisees the essence of true religion was rigorous keeping of the Sabbath; avoidance of anything or anyone that would make them unclean (i.e., "sinners"—tax collectors, women, Gentiles, etc.); careful observance of the regulations regarding fasting and ceremonial washing; and dutiful tithing and sacrifice.

The Witness of John the Baptizer (John 3:22–36)

The Study Guide does not comment on **John 3:22–36.** If you have time or if the class wants to consider this section, you may want to point out the selflessness of John the Baptizer. It is the mark of a great person to be willing to take a back seat to another. In this case John gave up his own "popularity" in order to point to Jesus.

Jesus and the Woman at the Well (John 4:1–42)

These verses outline the conversation between Jesus and a Samaritan woman. It was a surprising encounter. The Jews hated the Samaritans. The hostility between them went back hundreds of years. Because the Samaritans had intermarried with Gentiles, the Jews considered them half-breeds and traitors, worse than Gentiles. Many Jews refused to set foot on Samaritan soil and detoured around the country when traveling between Judea and Galilee.

Another point to keep in mind is the low estate of women among the Jews at our Lord's time. A strict Hebrew man would not even speak to his own wife or daughter in public. They had a saying: "Each time a man prolongs conversation with a woman he causes evil to himself, and desists from the law, and in the end inherits Gehinnom (destruction)." The male Jew began each day with a traditional prayer in which he thanked God for, among other things, the fact that he was neither a Gentile nor a woman. The rabbis used to debate whether women even had souls. Mindful of these attitudes we can understand better how exceptional it was for Jesus to talk to a Samaritan woman. Jesus was no racist or chauvinist. He began the first equal-rights and civil-rights movements by offering salvation to everyone, regardless of gender or genetics.

Searching the Scriptures

The Interview with Nicodemus (John 3:1–21)

1. See notes under "What's Going On Here."

2. The fact that Nicodemus came to Jesus "at night" may have special meaning because night and darkness have deep symbolical significance. Perhaps Nicodemus was afraid to be seen talking to Jesus, or he may have simply sought a quiet time. But *darkness* and *night* are sinister words in the gospel of John. They are often descriptive of the forces that are

opposed to God and God's Christ. The conversation with Nicodemus ends with a discussion about those who prefer darkness to the light. John does not record if Nicodemus remained "in the dark" or if he stepped into the light of salvation offered by Jesus.

3. Nicodemus was confused by Jesus' words. Like most Pharisees, he was looking for an earthly answer. Instead, Jesus gave him a spiritual answer: rebirth comes through water (Baptism) and the Holy Spirit. The new life is not one that will end in death, but one that will last forever.

4. The expression "so the Son of Man must be *lifted up* **(3:14, emphasis added)** refers to Jesus being lifted up on the cross. However, the phrase is also used in the New Testament to refer to Jesus' ascension. The two events seem to be so different but actually they are closely related. The only way to the glory of the Father is through the cross. The way to exaltation is the crucifixion. Indeed, John would have us realize that the crucifixion is Jesus' exaltation. Instead of defeat, the cross becomes crowning victory.

5. **John 3:16** takes us into the very heart of God. It tells us that He is a God who loves us even though we don't deserve His love. It tells us that His love encompasses the entire world. No one is excluded. It tells us that God's love is not just an emotion. It is God in action. He did not sit back, waiting for us to return to Him. God took the initiative. It tells us that He so desperately wants us to share His life that He gave up what was most precious to Him—His Son—for us.

The Woman at the Well (John 4:1–42)

1. See notes under "What's Going On Here."

2. Jesus exposes the Samaritan woman's past to His light—she knows that she is a sinner. She needs to get right with God. She wants to offer a sacrifice for her sin. She tries to trap the Jew sitting before her with a question about where must she go to do that **(4:20).** The Samaritans claimed the temple on Mount Gerizim was where God must be worshiped. The Jews claimed that Jerusalem was where one must go. In effect, she is asking Jesus, "Where is God to be found?"

Jesus replies that God is not some*place.* God is Spirit—with us everywhere we go. Worship does not depend on going to a certain place and going through certain motions. Worship is hearing God's truth as presented in His Word and responding with a thankful spirit. The example of Jesus and the experience of Christians throughout history suggest that we will find it helpful to set aside a specific place and stated times for formal worship with others, but God invites us to pray to Him at all times and everywhere.

3. The way the Samaritan woman addresses Jesus indicates her conversion. First she refers to Jesus rather caustically as "a Jew." When she thinks she may be able to be helped by Him she calls Him "Sir." Next, she comes to the realization that He is someone special, perhaps a "prophet." And finally, she confesses Him to be none other than "the Christ."

The Word for Us

Again, the discussion questions are to help relate the message of this portion of John's gospel to ourselves. Our encounter with Christ changes us. It changes our attitude toward ourselves, toward Christ, and toward other people.

1. The Good News of salvation is a message of hope for us in our need. Encourage the class to share something about the personal traps that might make them want to despair of ever being able to change. The kinds of problems are many—what they have in common is our inability to *fix* them by ourselves. We need the *victory*—the power of salvation in Jesus Christ. Talk about how the forgiveness we have allows us to begin each day anew and how the promise of ultimate victory we have makes it possible for us to deal with our internal traps in a positive and constructive way. Discuss ways in which Christians can share each others' pain and offer one another strength and hope.

2. It is the first step in being a witness to be able to say what faith means in a personal way. Encourage the class members to try to express their faith in Christ in their own words. Encourage their attempts. Make the sharing positive. Thank those who are willing to speak.

3. Allow the class to suggest ways in which we can, as individuals and as congregations, do a better job of dealing equally with people. Our pride and our prejudices make it very difficult for us to imitate the acceptance of Christ. What prejudgments and antagonisms do we need to repent of? What does the fact that God loves us even when we are unlovable say about our attitude toward others?

Closing

Follow the suggestion in the Study Guide. Then lead the group in a prayer, thanking God the Father for the precious gift of His Son and asking the Spirit to keep your hearts in faith.

Lesson 4
You Can't Do That! (John 4:43–5:47)

Before the Session

Carefully read through **John 4:43–5:47,** making note of any passages you want to share with the class participants. Also read through the Third Commandment and Luther's explanation.

The Third Commandment
Remember the Sabbath day by keeping it holy.
What does this mean? We should fear and love God so that we do not despise preaching and His Word, but hold it sacred and gladly hear and learn it.

What does this commandment mean for you? How does it apply to your life?

As always, arrive at your teaching area early to check the comfort level and the availability of Bibles.

Getting Started

Introduce any new class members. Begin with a prayer based on the Third Commandment, such as this: **Dear God in Heaven, we fear You because we have sinned against You. We love You because You have forgiven us through Jesus Christ. Guide us by Your Spirit as we get to know You better through Your Word. Give us joyful hearts to thank and worship You at all times. Amen.** Then have volunteers read the "Theme Verse" and "Goal."

What's Going On Here

This portion of the gospel is not too long to read in class. Perhaps participants could take turns reading a section at a time. The material in the Study Guide and the additional background information below could serve as comment.

The "royal official" **(4:46)** was probably an officer in Herod's service. As such, he must have had to swallow his pride to travel 20 miles from Capernaum to Cana to seek help from a traveling Jewish carpenter. It took great faith to return home with nothing but Jesus' assurance that his son would live. The ending of this episode brings to mind similar accounts in Acts in which entire Gentile families were converted **(Acts 16:33; 18:8)** and especially the case of another officer, Cornelius **(Acts 10).**

John 5 introduces another occasion on which Jesus clashed with the

Pharisees because of their inflexible observance of the Sabbath law. It is important to realize that our Lord did not set out to antagonize the Jewish leaders nor was it His intention to purposely violate tradition. He regularly worshiped in the synagogue **(Luke 4:16)**. John reports that Jesus often went to Jerusalem for major religious festivals. But Jesus was not a legalist. In **Mark 2:27** he states, "The Sabbath was made for man, not man for the Sabbath. So the Son of Man is Lord even of the Sabbath." Jesus knew that God had decreed the Sabbath rest for man's good. Jesus also saw that the mechanical application of God's Law could result in the opposite of what God intended, preventing help when help was needed. In such a situation Jesus never hesitated for a moment. He did the good He knew God intended (see **Mark 3:1–6**).

Searching the Scriptures

Acts of Healing (John 4:43–5:18)

1. In **4:50** we are told that "the man took Jesus at His word." He trusted that what Jesus told him was true—that Jesus was reliable and that his son would get well. In **4:53** his belief is not in what Jesus said but in Jesus Himself. He believes not simply that Jesus is trustworthy but that He is who He claims to be, God's Son.

2. The man had been an invalid for 38 years. Perhaps he had come to terms with his condition. Even in sickness, sometimes change is more difficult than the condition itself. Some people who are sick make demands on others that they never could if they were well. It is pleasant to be catered to and waited on. For all their protestations, they enjoy being sick.

3. The healed man couldn't keep the good news to himself. He had to tell everybody—even the Jews who were looking for a reason to get rid of Jesus.

4. Jesus contends in **5:17** that God did not stop working on the Sabbath. He continues to support and care for His creation at all times. Otherwise the world would return to the chaos from which God called it into existence. The argument for healing on the Sabbath is clear and, to the Pharisees, presumptuous: God shows love and care, even on the Sabbath—so can He.

The Discourse to the Jews (John 5:19–47)

1. In **5:19** Jesus identifies Himself as God's Son. As the *Son of God* He does not act on His own. Sonship means obedience, not independence. The function of the Son is to reproduce the action of the Father. Thus, Jesus declares that in healing on the Sabbath He is following God, not opposing Him. See **4:34; 6:38; 14:31**.

2. Jesus came to give life. He did that by restoring to full health the official's son and the invalid in Jerusalem. In **5:20–21** Jesus claims that the Father has given Him the power to grant life to whomever He will. These miracles, which lead to His discussion with the Jews, are dramatic declarations that Jesus' power over life and death is real. This power is applied to all who believe in the Father.

3. By "the dead" in **5:25,** Jesus appears to be referring both to those who are literally dead and to those who are spiritually dead. When Jesus raised Lazarus **(11:43)** He gave life to the physically dead. Those who come to faith and are given eternal life are the "raised" spiritually dead.

4. In **5:30** Jesus spoke of God as "Him who sent Me." The sending was His authorization. The testimony to His mission as Messiah was announced by the contemporary prophet John and also by the ancient prophets as recorded in Scripture **(5:39)**. The Pharisees failed to see this, however, and also failed to see the proof of His power was in the works that He did.

5. The word *study* in **John 5:39** can be translated either as a command (You *must* search the Scriptures) or as a statement of fact (You *do* search the Scriptures). The Jews pored over the pages of the Old Testament, confident that their diligent searching would reveal eternal life. But the key to the correct understanding of the Scriptures is Jesus Christ. Because the Jews failed to recognize Him as the Messiah, their lifelong preoccupation with the Scriptures was futile. It is possible to know much about the Bible without knowing the one thing needful: that Jesus Christ, God's Son, is our Savior.

6. The first five books of the Old Testament are often referred to by the name of their author, Moses. In a parable, Jesus told about the rich man and Lazarus **(Luke 16:19–31)**. In reply to the request of the rich man that Lazarus be sent from the dead to warn the man's brothers of the torments of hell, Abraham says, "They have Moses and the Prophets" **(Luke 16:29)**. He obviously meant that they could read about God's judgment in the writings of Moses and the Prophets. These writings of Moses were also known to the Jews as the *Torah* or *God's Law*. By telling the Jews they are setting their hopes on Moses, Jesus was pointing out their shortsightedness of believing that salvation can be achieved by keeping the Law. Jesus pointed out that the writings of Moses as a whole speak about Him. Since the Jews would not accept Moses' testimony to Jesus, it is not surprising that they would not accept Jesus' testimony to Himself.

The Word for Us

The first two discussion questions will give you and the class an opportunity to think again about the mission of the church that rises out of the Good News of salvation that John so clearly declares to us.

1. Try to avoid an argument about what is more important. Obviously both physical and spiritual needs are important and the Christian has a mission to respond to both. **James** clearly indicates in **chapter 2** that our faith shows itself in our mission to the whole person. The emphasis is on mission—on reaching out; on sharing the love of God in Christ.

2. The second question directs our attention to the contrast between the "offensive" message of Jesus and the timid way in which we sometimes speak and live the Gospel. The purpose is repentance and a new determination to confess boldly our faith.

3. With the last suggestion for discussion you might want to try a sharing session in which the members of the group express special ways in which this portion of Scripture has touched them. This should not be an occasion for sermonizing. The purpose is not to find "right" content in the interpretation of the passages but to give expression to the way these words of Christ have touched their own life. You might begin the discussion by revealing some special meaning here for you. Start by saying, "The words of Jesus in verse _____ have become special to me when I think of ..." Help the sharing to be open and positive. Take care not to reject anyone's attempts to share.

Closing

Follow the suggestion in the Study Guide. Then lead the class in prayer, asking God's Spirit to empower each of you as you go out to share the Good News with others.

Lesson 5

Bread Like You Never Had Before (John 6)

Before the Session

Read carefully through **John 6,** jotting down any notes and questions. Especially note what Jesus as the Bread of life means for you personally. Arrive early. Is your teaching area warm enough? cool enough? light enough? Are the chairs and tables set up? Make sure there are enough Bibles and pens or pencils.

Getting Started

Begin with a prayer, asking Jesus, the Bread of life, to come to your study group today and feed you with the nourishment of His Word. Ask members to keep in mind the properties of bread as they study today's lesson. Then have volunteers read the "Theme Verse" and "Goal."

What's Going On Here

You might begin this class by reading together **John 6:31–34,** which refers to *manna* and *bread*. Read also **6:3.** Challenge class members to tie together Jesus' going up on a mountainside, Moses, manna, and bread. Jesus is the new Moses. Moses went up the mountain to receive the Law. Jesus went up the mountain to speak the Gospel. Jesus is not manna that decays; He is the Bread of eternal life.

It should be noted that John devotes **chapters 13–17** to detailing what happened in the upper room on the night before Jesus was crucified. That is far more space than any of the other gospel writers give. Matthew, Mark, and Luke all include an account of the institution of the Lord's Supper in their rather brief record of Maundy Thursday events, but John omits it completely from his much fuller account. Instead, he speaks here (in **chapter 6**) of a special feeding.

Searching the Scriptures

The Feeding of the 5,000 (John 6:1–15)

1. Not everyone who followed Jesus came for religious reasons. Jesus was popular. The reputation He had made in Jerusalem preceded Him to Galilee. Some wanted to see the "celebrity"; some from Nazareth came out of local pride; and some hoped to see Him do something amazing—they wanted to be entertained, like Herod **(Luke 23:8).**

2. Andrew's evangelism efforts began in his family; he introduced his brother Simon Peter to Jesus. But we know from this passage that Andrew also told strangers and acquaintances about the wonderful Savior.

3. The parallels between the description of the feeding of the 5,000 and the institution of the Lord's Supper may indicate that John wants us to connect the two events.

4. In the Old Testament, God provided for His people's physical hunger. Now Jesus speaks of something greater—spiritual food that will last for an eternity.

Jesus Walking on the Water (John 6:16–21)

Jesus often referred to Himself as "I am" in the gospel of John. Here the emphasis is on the identification of Jesus with God—the God of the Old

Testament. The term will come up several times in this study.

Discourse on the Bread of Life (John 6:22–71)

1. Jesus was trying to help the people realize they were following Him for earthly gain, not because they sought the inner meaning of the miracles. They had seen the signs with their eyes but had not understood them.

2. In **6:27** Jesus was not condemning hard work and what it will buy; He was reminding us that "man does not live on bread alone, but on every word that comes from the mouth of God" **(Matthew 4:4)**. To *seal* means here "to validate." In the ancient world a seal was put on a document to ensure that it was authentic. At Jesus' Baptism God *sealed* Jesus by sending His Spirit upon Him **(1:33)**.

3. The people undoubtedly expected Jesus to give them a list of dos and don'ts **(6:28)**. They wanted guidance. The rules of the scribes and Pharisees were too complicated. They wanted a little shortcut. But their whole approach was wrong. They were looking for the *work* that would satisfy God. In **6:29** Jesus turned the normal meaning of the word *work* upside down. The *work* God wants from us is faith, which is not a work at all in the ordinary sense of that word. Faith is not an activity that we perform that makes us acceptable to God. It is, rather, the work of the Spirit through the Word by the grace of God. But the people still didn't understand; they wanted to barter with Jesus for miraculous signs in exchange for their work.

4. Here are some things that **John 6:35–40** indicates:

a. Jesus promises to satisfy our basic need.

b. Faith in Him is all we need.

c. God works the process of our believing.

d. Jesus has come from God to do God's will.

e. God's will is that no one given to Jesus by the Father will be lost.

f. God wants all people to believe in Jesus and have eternal life.

g. On the Last Day Jesus will raise up all those who believe in Him.

5. In **6:46** Jesus made a statement about Himself that had to astound His listeners. It was an axiom of the Jewish faith that no one had seen God. The Old Testament stated that no one could see God and live. Even statues and pictures attempting to represent God were forbidden. Yet Jesus stated that He had seen God.

6. **John 6:53–57** and **Matthew 26:26–29** are similar in wording. **John 6** speaks of *spiritual* in contrast to physical **(6:26)** eating and drinking, whereas Matthew 26 speaks of *sacramental* eating and drinking, which takes place only in the Sacrament of the Altar.

7. The disciples found what Jesus said to be "a hard teaching" **(6:60)**

not in the sense that it was hard to understand, but that it was hard to accept. They knew well enough that Jesus was saying that He was the very life of God and that He was sent by the Father. They did not lack perception but commitment.

8. **John 6:63–65** tells us that it is the function of the Holy Spirit to give us life. He does this by creating in us faith in Jesus Christ. Faith takes hold of the life the Father offers through His Son.

The Word for Us

1. Everyone struggles with doubt. Sometimes we deal with doubt by pretending it is not there. Often the pretending only makes the doubting worse. You might take time to let your class share some of their doubt—or their times of doubt. Just saying the problem out loud is helpful to many people. Work for an accepting attitude in the group that will allow the members to share without feeling "silly" or "wrong." You might encourage discussion by relating something of your own struggle with doubt or some incident that made you doubt the presence and reality of God in your life.

2. There is a temptation to try to manipulate God with our goodness. "Why," we say (remembering that we have been very good and have tried to do the right thing) "does this bad thing happen to me," or "Why doesn't God give me what I want and need?" We are tempted to make God our spiritual errand boy. Discuss these faith problems with your class. Encourage them to trust the goodness of God and the promises of Christ even when it seems that God is ignoring them or that He will not answer them. Again, don't find fault or reject anyone's expression of difficulty with their faith. An open atmosphere can be very healing for those who are struggling with their relationship to God.

Closing

Follow the suggestion in the Study Guide. Then lead the class in prayer, thanking God for the nourishment of His Word provided through your study, and asking Jesus, the Bread of life, to feed your faith every day with the promises of forgiveness and eternal life.

Lesson 6
Hostility Grows (John 7–8)

Before the Session

Read through **John 7–8.** As you do so, think about times when you would have liked to "disown" God. Perhaps you wanted to live contrary to what God desires. Perhaps you felt that God had let you down. What steps did you take to come back to God? Remember these experiences as you lead the discussion about the growing hostility toward Jesus.

As usual, check out the comfort level of the classroom before the session begins.

Getting Started

Open the session with a prayer, asking God to forgive you for the times you have turned away from Him, and granting you an open heart to hear, learn, and live His Word. Then have volunteers read the "Theme Verse" and "Goal."

What's Going On Here

It may be well to begin the class by reading through this section together in the Study Guide. It will be a review of the events for those who have read through the section at home and will set the stage for the closer look for those who have not. The emphasis is on the continued action of Jesus and His words that claim His Messiahship and the continued misunderstanding and hostility of His enemies.

Searching the Scriptures
Jesus at the Feast of Tabernacles (John 7)

1. The brothers of Jesus, like His mother in **2:1–11,** wanted to tell Jesus how to act. They saw the signs that He did but could not understand their meaning. We have a saying: "Familiarity breeds contempt." That seems to be true of Jesus' own family. They were too close to Him to view Him as anyone other than their son and brother. His brothers wanted Him to perform miracles in Jerusalem so He would get wider exposure and greater publicity. Perhaps they felt that His renown would somehow reflect on them. Jesus refused them.

2. A basic principle of education is that we learn by doing. You can read all the books you want to about the things of this world—swimming or motor maintenance or cooking, etc., but you will not really learn how to do

any of those things until you put the books down and jump in the water, open the hood, or turn on the stove. But in our relationship to God, He is our teacher **(8:31–32; 14:26)** and knowledge comes as we meditate on His Word **(Ps. 1:2)** and follow Him.

3. **Leviticus 12:3** says, "On the eighth day [after birth] the boy is to be circumcised." For many, the eighth day would fall on the Sabbath. The Pharisees not only allowed circumcision on the Sabbath but taught that it was especially blessed. If they condoned circumcision on the Sabbath why did they condemn Jesus for healing on the Sabbath?

4. There was a popular belief among the Jews that the Messiah already existed but was being kept hidden until the time God wanted Him to appear. He would come among people suddenly and no one would know where He had come from. The Jews knew that Jesus had grown up in Nazareth. They knew His parents and family. Therefore, they argued that He could not be the Messiah.

5. When Jesus talked about leaving and going to a place to which the Jews could not follow, He was referring to His ascension into heaven, His return to power at the right hand of the Father. The Jews had been scattered because of their captivity by the Assyrians and the Babylonians centuries earlier. Not all returned to Palestine after their captors fell from power. Other Jews earned their living as traders and lived throughout the ancient world. The *dispersion* is a technical term for the Jews who lived anywhere else but in Palestine. The term *Greeks* commonly referred to Gentiles regardless of their nationality.

6. **Verse 39** in the best Greek manuscripts reads: "For as yet there was no Spirit." That does not mean that the Spirit did not exist but that the full power of God's Spirit was not yet given to God's people. Pentecost could not occur before Good Friday and Easter Sunday. After Jesus performed His saving work, the Holy Spirit became powerful among people in a way not seen before.

The Woman Caught in Adultery (John 8:1–11)

1. The Pharisees betrayed their basic attitude toward people in their treatment of the woman caught in the act of adultery. They did not view her as a person at all. It is always wrong to treat persons as things. That is a very real temptation for each of us. We live in a world of terrible impersonality and loneliness.

2. The older accusers left first because they were most conscious of their past failures. The older we get the more difficult it becomes to hide from the enormity of our sins.

3. Jesus did not condone or excuse what the woman had done. He was

not abandoning judgment, just deferring sentence. Jesus was not "soft" on adultery. Rather, He forgave the sinner. He neither destroyed her with punishment (as the Pharisees would have done) nor excused her as if her act made no difference.

The Witness of the Father (John 8:12–59)

1. **Verses 31–32** tell us that

a. belief in Jesus is essential to becoming His disciple;

b. to remain a disciple means to abide in His Word—to constantly listen to, learn from, and be obedient to it;

c. discipleship results in knowledge of the truth—the truth about Jesus, about God, and about ourselves;

d. the truth that discipleship reveals makes us free—free from sin, free from ourselves, and free for serving others.

2. The Jews relied on their formal family relationship to Abraham. They trusted that the promises of God to Abraham and his descendants were automatically theirs. The freedom Jesus offered seemed irrelevant to them.

3. In **8:51** Jesus noted that the person who receives Him has already escaped death. We have passed from death into life. When we end our existence on earth we do not really die. We merely pass from life into life.

4. The key to **8:12, 24–25, 58** is the phrase *I am*. In these two little words, Jesus claimed to be God. He said that He was in existence before Abraham was born. He is the eternal *I am*. See **1:1–3**. The Jews tried to stone Him because they understood what Jesus was saying.

The Word for Us

1. The first item is an important topic for discussion in the church. We add a great number of rules to our religion in the church and in the individual congregation. Good order dictates that we obey the rules. The purpose of this discussion is not to find fault with the rules or to try to write better rules—it is to come to an understanding about the purpose of rules. Rules set limits. They establish order. They cease to be helpful when they do injury to people. The Pharisees were interested in the rule. Jesus was interested in the person. Discuss ways in which rules can be made more responsive to the needs of people, and the way good rules serve people.

2. In spite of the fact that we live in a free country we are constantly enslaved—by our habits and weaknesses, by the attitudes of other people, by social pressures and the like. What does the freedom of the Gospel mean to those enslavements? Encourage the class to be honest about the personal or social traps that rob them of their freedom. Don't just com-

plain about them. Speak the Good News of salvation to the pain of the enslavement. Ultimately, in Christ, we are victorious over everything that would seek to enslave us. Share the confidence and hope that our faith in Christ can give us—even when we feel trapped and less than free.

Closing

Follow the suggestion in the Study Guide. Close with a prayer, perhaps using the words of **Mark 9:24:** "I do believe; help me overcome my unbelief!"

Lesson 7

The Shepherd and His Sheep (John 9–10)

Before the Session

To prepare for today's lesson, you may wish to do some research into the nature of sheep and shepherds. What is the character of sheep? What kind of care do they need? What are some dangers exclusive to sheep? What sort of duties do shepherds perform?

Also, as usual, check out the comfort of your classroom, and make sure you have a supply of extra Bibles and pencils for the participants.

Getting Started

Begin your class session with a prayer to the Good Shepherd. Ask Him to heal the blindness of your sinful hearts and to prepare them for the healing balm of His Word. Thank Him for His guidance and protection as your Shepherd. Then have volunteers read the "Theme Verse" and "Goal."

What's Going On Here

Chapters 9 and 10 present portions of John's gospel that will be quite familiar to some of the class. **Chapter 10:1–16** in particular is a favorite of many because it presents the comforting picture of Jesus as the Good Shepherd. To introduce the class to the lesson, you might read these verses together aloud. Ask the participants how the words make them feel. What comfort or hope do they get from this portion of Scripture? As you begin the lesson, compare the reaction of the group with the hostility of the Pharisees. Why were they hostile? Review briefly the events of **chapters 7** and **8** and lead into the healing in **chapter 9.**

Searching the Scriptures

The Man Born Blind (John 9)

1. Many people of our Lord's day thought that all suffering was divine punishment for sin. The disciples' question indicates that they accepted this common superstition. They were not alone; even today there are people who believe this. Jesus rejected the notion that the man's blindness was punishment for a sin that the man or his parents had committed. There is, of course, a sense in which all suffering is caused by sin. The Bible indicates that suffering and sin are related, as are death and sin. But we cannot assume that a particular sin results in a specific misfortune.

2. Jesus was aware that His time was limited. The night and the powers of darkness would close in on Him soon enough. He is the light **(9:5)**. While He was on earth it was day. He could not put off helping the man born blind because it was the Sabbath and because the Pharisees might take offense. It was precisely to do such works that the Father had sent Him into the world.

3. The Pharisees were divided in their assessment of Jesus **(9:16)**. With clear logic each side came to an exactly opposite conclusion. One said: The Sabbath rest was commanded by God; Jesus was breaking the Sabbath; therefore He could not be from God. The other group said: No person can perform miracles unless God is with him or her; Jesus was performing miraculous cures; therefore God must be with Him.

4. Since the Pharisees could not get the reply they wanted from the man whom Jesus healed **(9:17)**, they turned to his parents. They hoped that it would turn out that the man was either not their son and so a fake, or that he was not really blind since birth, or that there was some natural explanation to his recovery of sight **(9:18–23)**. In order to press their point and retain the upper hand over the people, they refused to admit to the synagogue anyone who acknowledged Jesus as the Christ. This would be the modern-day Christian equivalent of being excommunicated; a very shameful experience.

5. The Pharisees wanted the man born blind to repudiate his testimony that Jesus healed him. They had declared Jesus "a sinner," that is, one who did not scrupulously observe all the ritual laws that the scribes had established. The man simply refused to comment on their evaluation of Jesus. All he could declare from firsthand experience was what happened to him. He told them very simply and directly the effect that Jesus had on his life.

Discuss with your class the implications of this kind of *witnessing*. What makes it effective?

6. We saw in **chapter 4** how the terms that the Samaritan woman used

in speaking to Jesus reflected her gradually changing appreciation of who He is. We can see the same kind of progression here. In **9:11** the man born blind refers to the Lord simply as "the man they call Jesus." In **9:17** he says, "He is a prophet." In **9:35** the expression "Son of Man" (some manuscripts have "Son of God") is introduced. The development reaches its climax in **9:38:** "The man said, 'Lord, I believe,' and he worshiped Him."

Jesus the Good Shepherd (John 10)

1. In **10:3–5** Jesus tells us the following:

a. Those that belong to Him listen to what He has to say. They are attentive to His Word.

b. Jesus knows us intimately. We are separate, distinct individuals to Him, with names that He knows.

c. Jesus is the one who chooses us. He calls us to be His. He seeks the lost and the erring.

d. Jesus does not send us out into the world alone. He goes with us. More than that, He goes ahead of us to show us the way.

e. We are really His only if we follow Him. We demonstrate that we have heard His voice not by repeating His words but by obeying His directions.

2. When the Palestinian shepherd kept his sheep out in the fields during the warm summer months, he would bring them together at night into a roofless enclosure made up of a low encircling wall. This *sheepfold* had an opening at one point that served as the entry or exit. There was no special *gate* or door. After the sheep were led into the enclosure the shepherd would lie down in the opening so that the sheep could not get out and no one could get in without his knowing it. In that way the shepherd actually became the door of the sheepfold.

3. In **10:8** Jesus is referring to the self-serving shepherds that Ezekiel spoke about, and particularly their contemporary counterparts in His day, the scribes and Pharisees.

4. The "other sheep" of **10:16** refer to the Gentiles. Jesus is the Savior of the world **(4:42).** He is concerned about all people, though most of His earthly ministry was directed toward the Jews. See Paul's expression of this in **Galatians 3:28** and **Ephesians 2:11–12.**

5. Jesus had been performing miracles according to what the Father had foretold in Scripture. The fulfillment of the Father's words show that Jesus is the Messiah. See **Luke 7:19–23.**

6. John the Baptizer's function was to ready the world for Jesus. He was to proclaim the coming of the King and to identify Him. He was not the Messiah, as some of his followers thought. He did no miracles.

The Word for Us

The material in this section would be most meaningful for class members if you could encourage them to participate in a discussion about how the comfort and hope of these words speak to them as individuals. The paragraphs in the Study Guide offer some suggestions about how you might begin such a sharing session. You might want to allow a free discussion, especially of **chapter 10,** to encourage the sharing of personal assurance.

1. This question encourages participants to compare the sufferings of the blind man with the sufferings they have learned from. Suffering tends either to destroy or to strengthen. Often it is the attitude of the sufferer that determines the result. Make the sharing positive. Let it lend hope to those who are undergoing difficulty. The blind man did not give up hope. **John 10** gives us great reason for hope in the personal, everlasting love and care of Christ.

2. This question deals with loneliness, which can cause us to forget God's love and promises. Encourage participants to find verses in **John 10** from which they can find comfort during times of loneliness.

3. Certain kinds of pain often cause us to despair of God's love. For many, grief is a devastating experience. Share how the words of **John 10** take on special meaning at special times.

Closing

Follow the suggestion in the Study Guide. Close with a prayer thanking Jesus, our Good Shepherd, for always watching over and protecting His sheep. Encourage participants to join in the prayer with specific thanksgivings or requests.

Lesson 8

The Resurrection and the Life (John 11)

Before the Session

Read through John 11 and take notes of how this section pertains to you personally. Make sure the room is comfortable and that there are extra Bibles and pens or pencils available.

Getting Started

Begin the session with a prayer, asking God to guide your study today. Then have volunteers read the "Theme Verse" and "Goal."

What's Going On Here

Verses 28–44 of this chapter give a brilliant and beautiful picture of Jesus as man (He wept) and God (He raised Lazarus). As an introduction to today's class you may wish to read through these verses together or read the introductory material in the Study Guide and then go through the whole chapter quickly before getting to the discussion questions below.

Searching the Scriptures

1. We should expect that Mary and Martha would have asked Jesus to heal Lazarus, or at the very least to come as quickly as He could. They apparently knew Him so well and were so confident of His love for them and their brother that they did not feel it necessary to ask His help.

2. Lazarus did die; but Jesus knew what He would do. This would not be death for Lazarus in the same final sense that death is normally. This death would result in renewed life shortly.

3. In the second half of **11:4** Jesus appears to be using words in more than one sense, as John records Him doing elsewhere in the gospel. First, He means to say that the illness of Lazarus would give the Father an opportunity to show forth His *glory* through His Son by the miracle that Jesus would perform with the Father's power. Second, since the *glory* of Jesus begins with the cross, **11:4** can also be seen as an expression by our Lord that He knew the ultimate consequence of raising Lazarus. He knew that this miracle would galvanize His opponents, and the result would be His own death.

4. It has been suggested that Jesus waited two days before going to Bethany so that there would be no doubt about the fact that Lazarus was really dead when He arrived. His delay would make the miraculous sign all the more impressive.

5. In **11:11** Jesus said, "Our friend Lazarus has *fallen asleep*" (emphasis added). As the other biblical references indicate, in order to express their firm conviction that death is not the end of man's existence, the New Testament writers commonly spoke of death as *sleep*. It is interesting to note that the word *cemetery* comes from the same Greek word for "sleep" that is used here. For the Christian a cemetery is not a final resting place, but, as its name implies, only a sleeping place, a dormitory.

6. In **11:15** Jesus did not say that He was glad that Lazarus had died but that He was glad He was not there when it happened. The miraculous sign

He was going to perform would help to strengthen their faith. It was to the disciples' advantage that Jesus was absent. He knew that what He intended to do would have dire consequences for Him; but it would fix their faith in Him more firmly than ever.

7. John emphasized that Lazarus had been dead for four days in order to stress the incredible nature of this miraculous sign that Jesus performed.

8. In **11:21–22** Martha expressed her confidence that if Jesus had been present He could have prevented Lazarus' death. Further, she was confident that He and the Father are *one*, as Jesus claims, and that even though Lazarus was dead and buried Jesus could still pray to the Father for help and the Father would answer Him. Discuss some of the implications for our own death that the confidence of Jesus in the face of death—and Lazarus' resurrection—have for us. Why is death no longer a real threat to us?

9. As we read the gospels it is good to be alert to the significance of acts, gestures, places, etc. Mary's falling at Jesus' feet **(11:32)** is usually recognized and understood for what it is, an act of worship; but we do not always note the significance of gestures, like Jesus' touching people **(Mark 1:41)**; or the locale in which an event occurs, like the fact that the feeding of the 5,000 took place on a mountainside **(John 6:3)**; or the presence of people and things, like the cloud that indicated the presence of God at the Transfiguration **(Mark 9:7)**.

10. Jesus prayed **(11:41–42)** because He did not act on His own, and He wanted the people to know it. He acted out of the power given Him by the Father. (If Jesus had *needed* to pray as often as He did, what does that say about *our* need to pray?)

11. The Sadducees were wealthy, aristocratic members of Jewish society. They were very much involved in politics and collaborated with the Romans to maintain their position of power. When Jesus attacked the business going on in the temple **(2:13–17)** He hit them where it hurt the most, in their pocketbooks. Furthermore, the Sadducees did not believe that there was a life after death **(Mark 12:18–23)** so Jesus' claim to be "the resurrection and the life" would be doubly obnoxious to them.

12. The Sanhedrin, represented by their leader, Caiaphas, was concerned only about the retention of its prestige, power, and position.

13. In **11:49–50** Caiaphas counseled a course of pure political expediency. He was not interested in the theological question some of the Sanhedrin were debating. Caiaphas had no interest in such subtleties. He was a power broker. For him the issue was simple: Either Jesus goes or they will go. He feared the Romans and knew that a political upheaval would be his downfall. In 70 A.D. his fears were realized and Jerusalem was

destroyed by the Romans. Caiaphas was interested in self-preservation, but viewed from the counsels of God, Caiaphas' statement is the grandest truth ever spoken, for it is the expression of God's purpose in sending His Son into the world. It is the Gospel proclaimed by the most unlikely and unwitting evangelist.

14. The *other sheep* that Jesus referred to in **10:16** are those who are not of the nation of Israel. They are the Gentiles, "the scattered children of God" **(11:52).**

15. Jesus left Jerusalem because His hour had not yet come. He was not afraid. He would be back—and soon. Though it would not appear to be the case, He would be in control of events. He would be delivered into the hands of His enemies according to His Father's time and not His enemies'.

The Word for Us

These discussion questions give you the opportunity to deal with specific problems that may have troubled or may be in the minds of class members.

1. This question could be a continuation of your discussion on grief from last session. It could be a way of coming to agreement on some positive suggestions for dealing with death and funerals. Connect the discussion with the promise of **John 11** and the confidence in the faith of life after death expressed by Mary and Martha in this chapter. You might make a list of some of the funeral customs in your community (viewing the body, family gatherings, flowers, graveside service, memorial service, etc.) in light of our Christian faith and the Christ we know from John's gospel. Are they helpful? Why or why not?

2. This question deals with one of the ways that our faith is tested. Sometimes the pressure of those around us makes it difficult for us to say what we believe and to defend it. Make this a time in which the people of your class can share some of those difficult times. Perhaps you might have to lead the discussion by retelling an experience of your own in which you found it difficult to speak up for your faith. Be positive and accepting.

Closing

Follow the suggestion in the Study Guide. Close with a prayer, thanking Jesus for the full life He grants, both now and after death.

Lesson 9
The Final Trip to Jerusalem (John 12–13)

Before the Session
Read through these two chapters, making note of some of the ways you have been blessed and served by the Lord and also of things for which you want to praise God. As usual, check out your room ahead of time. Make sure you have extra Bibles and pens available.

Getting Started
Begin your session with a prayer, praising Jesus for all His gifts of life, love, peace, and joy. Have volunteers read the "Theme Verse" and "Goal."

What's Going On Here
In order to begin this section you might want to start your class by reading **12:1–8** and **13:1–17** aloud, either in unison, or ask for volunteers. Spend a little time comparing the two passages. What message did the washing of the feet convey? Why was Mary's washing so special? According to the examples of Jesus and Mary what should be our attitude toward fellow believers? In what way do we "wash their feet"? How do we "wash Jesus' feet" today? After discussing this, read through the paragraphs under this section in the Study Guide.

Searching the Scriptures
The Last Week (John 12)
1. **Luke 10:38–42** tells about another time when Martha served Jesus. On that occasion she was rebuked by Him because of what she was doing. She might have said to herself: "Well, if that's the way He wants it, let Him see if I put myself out for Him again!" But Martha was not such a small-minded person. She did not nurse hurt feelings. And so here in **John 12** we find her doing what she did best, serving Jesus with her hands.

John made a point to mention that Lazarus was there, reclining at the table with Jesus. This may have been mentioned to quell the skepticism of any who did not believe that Jesus had raised Lazarus from the dead.

Mary gave Jesus a most precious gift. It would have taken a day laborer an entire year to earn enough money to buy what she poured on Jesus' feet. Mary's love did not count the cost. She did for Him what none of the Twelve had ever done; what, in fact, He later did for them in the upper room.

Judas Iscariot was a man whose outlook was so warped that he measured everything with dollar signs. What Jesus called a memorable act of love Judas viewed as a wasteful extravagance. He was supposed to be in control of the group's money, but it was in control of him.

2. Jesus' entire life was devoted to helping the poor, the outcast, the sick, the leper, the powerless. His response in **12:8** must be seen in its context. He was saying to Judas: "Friend, don't worry. If you are really concerned about the poor, you will have the rest of your life to show it. My days are numbered—as you know well enough. If you want to show love to Me, do it now." Was His response not only a rebuke but also a veiled attempt by Jesus to reach out to Judas and call him from the path that was leading him toward betrayal? Discuss the question.

3. In **Zechariah 9:9** we read: "See, your king comes to you, *righteous and having salvation, gentle* and riding on a donkey, on a colt, the foal of a donkey" (emphasis added). Jesus is a righteous, triumphant king, but also a gentle, humble king. He was not the kind of king the crowds wanted, not the kind of king they thought they were cheering. His kingdom is "not of this world" **(John 18:36).** When a king went out to war he rode on a horse. When he came in peace he rode a donkey. Jesus is the humble Prince of peace.

4. In **12:19** the Pharisees were exaggerating their predicament. Jesus was gaining more and more support. There was nothing they could do to blunt His popularity. Although an exaggeration of their present situation, their words were an accurate prophecy of what was to happen. Jesus is the Savior of the world, as the Samaritans had declared **(4:42).**

5. The Greeks mentioned in **12:20–22** were the immediate fulfillment of the truth of the Pharisees' statement **(12:19).** They were an indication and a prediction that the Gospel will go out to all the world, and that the world will come to Jesus.

6. In **12:24–26** Jesus was saying that life comes only through death. That was true for Him. It is equally true for us.

7. God the Father spoke at Jesus' baptism and His transfiguration to announce the importance of the events. Now, as then, God speaks to emphasize the significance of what is about to happen.

8. **Verse 32** is explained in **verse 33.** Jesus was talking not about His ascension but His crucifixion, His being *lifted up* on the cross.

9. In **12:35–36** Jesus is talking about Himself. He is the Light of the world. That is why He said, "Put your trust in the light." He wanted them to know that He would not always be with them. In less than a week there would be darkness at midday.

10. These words are a free quotation of **Isaiah 6:9–10** and are quoted or

alluded to repeatedly in the New Testament **(Matthew 13:14–15; Mark 4:12; Luke 8:10; Acts 28:26–27; Romans 11:8; 2 Corinthians 3:14).** It is necessary to discover what these words meant in their original setting. God did not arbitrarily blind people's eyes and close their hearts. Isaiah was describing the reaction of the Israelites to his preaching. He cast his words in the form of a command, but meant them to be descriptive of the outcome of his prophesying: The Israelites refused to believe. Their sin was that they hardened their hearts. The result was that they were judged. Regardless of how we explain these verses, the entire Old and New Testaments stand in solid agreement that God dearly loves all people and wants no one to reject His offer of salvation in Jesus Christ. It is unthinkable that God would love the world so much that He would send His Son to die for it and then that He would intentionally exclude some from His grace. If a person does not believe, it is not God's fault. Those who refuse to believe are already judged. Hopefully, our study of the gospel of John to this point has left no doubt of the genuineness of our Lord's invitation and His desire that *everyone* come to Him.

11. Here are some of the dominant themes restated in **12:44–50:**

a. Jesus and God are one. Therefore, belief in Him is the same as belief in God.

b. Jesus is God's ambassador sent to our world.

c. To see Jesus is to see God and to know what God is like.

d. Jesus is the Light of the world. Belief in Him removes the darkness of death from our life.

e. Jesus did not come to condemn mankind; however, His second coming will result in condemnation for all who reject Him.

f. This world will end, and at that time judgment will be pronounced.

g. To listen to Jesus is to listen to God. Jesus is God's Word of good news in human form.

h. God's Word to mankind in Jesus Christ is eternal life.

An Object Lesson in Humility (John 13)

1. How would you feel and act if you knew you had only a few hours to live? Jesus knew that He would be dead before the evening of the following day. He also knew that He was returning to His rightful place with the Father. He might well have been distracted by fear or filled with contempt. Instead, He shows love to His disciples and looks out for them to the very end. Discuss the implications of Jesus' action for us in connection with the questions in the Study Guide and discussion question 2 under "The Word for Us."

2. We can fool ourselves into imagining that knowing what our Lord

wants us to do is somehow meritorious. Jesus told the story about the two sons who were ordered by their father to work in the fields. The truly obedient son was not the son who *said* that he would go (and did not), but the one who at first refused—and afterwards went.

3. Jesus told His disciples what was going to happen in advance of its occurrence so they would not be shocked into disbelief. He wanted them to know that He is God, despite how incredible that might seem to them when they witness His crucifixion.

4. With the departure of Judas, Jesus knew that the events that would end in His crucifixion were now set in motion. There was no turning back. It was as good as done.

5. Jesus' love is self-sacrificing, forgiving, totally accepting, all-encompassing. It must have been frustrating for Him to see how little His disciples seemed to understand what He tried to teach them. They argued over who was the greatest among them and who deserved the positions of power on His right hand and on His left, thinking that His kingdom was no different from any other. One betrayed Him. They all deserted Him. Yet He loved them completely. He understood their failings. His patience with them never wore thin.

The Word for Us

The discussion questions for this lesson would lead to consideration of the implications of discipleship today. Discipleship implies a way of life. It is a way of life that attempts to *imitate* Christ. Use this time to talk about what it might mean to *imitate* Christ in our world.

1. The discussion centers on *secret disciples*. Help class members to see that one cannot really be a *secret* disciple, even though there are situations in which it is very difficult to be an open and witnessing believer. In repenting of those failures, point again to the Gospel, which emphasizes the greatness of the act of God in Jesus Christ for us. We share not a *secret message* but the great *Good News* of God in Christ.

2. It is risky to love. There is a measure of risk in showing love. Christians are often taken advantage of when they try to help. Sometimes they are considered foolish for giving when everyone else is taking. After allowing discussion on the risk and the cost of loving, return to the example of Jesus. He took the risk unto death to love us.

3. The discussion of this question can be an open sharing about ways in which the love of Christ in us enables us to act toward people. You might encourage the members of your class to share their struggles to love and show love. What kinds of people are particularly hard to love? In what situations? Again, repentance and renewal in the message of the Gospel makes

it possible for us to return to our attempts to "follow" Jesus.

Closing

Follow the suggestion in the Study Guide. Then close with a prayer, thanking Jesus for His love and faithfulness, and asking the Holy Spirit to always keep you faithful and to give you strength to show the love of Jesus in every situation.

Lesson 10

When You Know You Are Going to Die
(John 14–15)

Before the Session

As you read through this section of Scripture before class, note the words of Jesus that comfort you, reassure you, or that you can apply to your life. Keep these notes handy as you teach; perhaps you could encourage the other participants to do the same. Don't forget to check the room setup before class.

Getting Started

Open with prayer. Ask Jesus to speak to your hearts as He spoke to His disciples. Then ask for volunteers to read the "Theme Verse" and "Goal."

What's Going On Here

As John reflected on the life of Jesus, he was moved by the Spirit to write, "Jesus knew that the time had come for Him to leave this world and go to the Father. Having loved His own who were in the world, He now showed them the full extent of His love" (13:1). Few things demonstrate the love of Jesus as powerfully as the opening verses of our lesson for this week. To begin the lesson for this week, read the familiar verses from 14:1–6 in unison. These verses set the tone of love and concern for the disciples that Jesus had as He faced His approaching death. Then read through the paragraph under this heading in the Study Guide. Spend a little time talking about the questions there; they will serve as a good introduction to the words of Jesus in these chapters.

Searching the Scriptures

Going Away to the Father (John 14)

1. If members of the class have different translations of the Bible, you will probably notice a variety of translations for **14:1–2.** The reason for the diversity is that there is no punctuation in the manuscripts (early Greek was not punctuated) so we cannot tell whether a question or a statement is intended. In any case, in **14:2** Jesus tells us that He goes to prepare a place for us. We do not have to be afraid of death, because we are not going into the unknown. We are not traveling to a strange and forbidding land. We will be met by our friend and Savior, who has gone ahead to make all the arrangements.

2. Jesus is *the Way* that leads all people to the Father, to heaven, to eternal life. The Christian faith was called *the Way*, as the passages in **Acts** show.

3. In **14:6** Jesus claims to be *the way* to God, *the truth* about God, and *the life* of God. In Him, and only in Him, we have access to the Father. In **14:10** He claims that He speaks as God gives Him authority, for God the Father is in Him and working through Him.

4. This verse contains Jesus' prediction and promise that after His ascension and because of it His followers would be empowered by the Holy Spirit to continue to heal and help people as He had done. They would be able to offer His forgiveness to sinners.

5. To pray in Jesus' name does not mean mechanically to end our prayer with that phrase, as though it is some kind of magic formula by which we can manipulate God to give us what we want. It means to pray about those things that we know are in accord with God's intention as revealed in Jesus. That rules out all selfish and vindictive requests. Basically all Christian prayer can be reduced to one petition, the prayer of Jesus Himself: "Not as I will, but as You will" **(Matthew 26:39).**

6. In **14:16** Jesus promises to send us "another *Counselor.*" The King James version translates as *Comforter.* The Greek word is *parakletos*, from which comes the expression *the Paraclete.* A *parakletos* was someone called in to help, for example, a witness called in to testify for someone on trial or lawyer called in to defend a person. The word *Comforter* comes from the same basic word, as does *fortitude.* The Holy Spirit is one who is called into our life not just to console us but to fortify us, to make us brave, to make us strong to do God's will. In **14:17** John speaks of the Holy Spirit as "the Spirit of truth." The Spirit's function is to reveal to us the truth about Jesus or, to express it another way, to reveal Jesus as the *Truth.* The function of the Holy Spirit is to bear witness to Jesus. Any

explanation of the Holy Spirit that separates the work of the Spirit from the work of Christ or which does not make the work of the Spirit complementary to the work of Christ is misleading.

7. One of the functions of the Holy Spirit is to bring to our remembrance the teaching of our Lord. Of all the encouragements for right living none is more powerful than the recollection of the example given us by Jesus. The Spirit is not a kind of cosmic encyclopedia of all knowledge. The "all things" (14:26) refers to all the things that Jesus said and did. The disciples did not understand much of Jesus' ministry until after His ascension (John 2:22; 12:16). Then, by the power of the Spirit working in them, they remembered and realized what He had done.

The True Vine (John 15)

1. Jesus emphasizes in 15:3 that we are *made clean*. We do not cleanse ourselves. It is Jesus who cleanses and purifies us through the word of forgiveness, that is, through Himself, who is the Word of forgiveness.

2. To "remain in" Jesus means simply to keep in contact with Him—to live by the power that He generates. We are branches that depend on the vine for our life source. We "remain in," that is, keep contact with Jesus as we allow Him to speak to us through His Word, as we receive His body and His blood in the Sacrament of the Altar, as we communicate with Him through prayer

3. If we abide in Jesus and His words are controlling and informing our lives, then our prayers will be prayers that God can unhesitatingly grant because they will be prayers submitted in keeping with God's will. Just as Jesus did not seek His own will but bowed before the will of His Father, so do we who call Jesus Lord.

4. As people with whom we come in contact notice the quality of life that God's Spirit generates in us, they will be led to ask what makes us act the way we do. Then we will have the opportunity to give the glory to God and witness to His Son.

5. We can hardly fail to be impressed with how often and in how many different ways Jesus stressed the necessity for obedience. The Christian is totally free. But the paradox of Christian freedom is that it is not the freedom to do what *we* want but to do what *God* wants. It is the freedom to enter voluntary servitude. It is, simply stated, the freedom to become like our Lord.

6. When we talk about faith in Christ, we must never lose sight of the central fact of Christian experience: it is not we who have chosen God but He who has chosen us. People say that they "have found God." If they have, it is only because God first found them (15:16). Our acceptance of

God is a response to His prior invitation. Our *finding* Him is a result of His having searched us out. As John says in his first epistle: "We love because He first loved us" **(1 John 4:19)**.

The Word for Us

The discussion questions give you and your class the opportunity to reflect on the message of the concern for His followers that Jesus expressed in this portion of the gospel.

1. Some misunderstand the promises of God in Christ and believe that if they have enough faith they will be able to be free from all trouble, fear, and doubt. They picture peace as the absence of anything disturbing. Christ's peace is assurance and hope even in the midst of trouble. The amount of ease we have is not a measure of the strength of our faith. Our peace comes by means of the gift of the power of the Spirit that makes us able to deal with those things that would rob us of peace.

2. When discussing the pruning done by God it is best to avoid trying to look for some hidden cause in every trouble that comes into a person's life. To be sure, some of the sharpness of life is permitted by God in order to prune us—strengthen us. But it does little good to try to figure out the causes of difficulty—it is more productive to look for the positive solutions to our dilemmas, drawing on the grace of God for the strength to overcome. We can be confident that things work together for our good, as stated in **Romans 8:28.**

3. As peace is not ease—neither is joy fun. Joy is the inner assurance that we belong to God and that nothing can overcome us or rob us of our home in heaven. Many things will interfere with our joy. Many times our life will not be fun. But we need to cling to the assurance that God desires for us to have joy. Help your class understand that our religion is not a gloomy duty to perform but the celebration of what God has done for us. Share ways in which the joy of faith has become clear, and suggest ways of expressing that joy in life.

Closing

Follow the suggestion in the Study Guide. Close with a prayer, thanking Jesus for the peace He gives and for sending the Holy Spirit, the Comforter, as a guide.

Lesson 11

When You Know You Are Going to Die (Continued) (John 16–17)

Before the Session

Read through these two chapters, taking notes as before. Make sure that your classroom is comfortable and in order.

Getting Started

Begin with a prayer, asking the Holy Spirit to open your hearts and minds to what you are about to learn. Then have volunteers read the "Theme Verse" and "Goal."

What's Going On Here

To introduce this lesson you might want to reread the paragraph under this heading in the Study Guide for lesson 10 along with the paragraph in this lesson. These will set the time, place, and tone of this portion of Scripture—a continuation of the last discourse of Jesus to His disciples shortly before His death.

Searching the Scriptures

Prediction of Things to Come (John 16)

1. Paul believed he was serving God when he expelled believers in Jesus from the synagogues, persecuted them for their beliefs, imprisoned and even put to death those who would not renounce their faith.

2. While Jesus was in human form He limited Himself—voluntarily—to the restrictions of time and space that affect every human being. As our risen Savior He operates under no such limitations. It is possible for Him to be with His disciples at all times and in all places. Through the abiding presence of the Holy Spirit, who testifies about Jesus **(15:26)**, the promise of Jesus is fulfilled: "Surely I am with you always, to the very end of the age" **(Matthew 28:20).**

3. *Righteousness*, particularly the righteousness of God **(Romans 1:17),** is a key concept in the letters of St. Paul. The righteousness of which the Holy Spirit will convince the world **(16:10)** is Jesus Christ's righteousness—that He was the innocent, righteous Son of God as He claimed and that through His death, resurrection, and ascension the righteousness of God is available to all those who believe in Jesus as their Lord and Savior.

4. The *judgment* referred to in **16:11** is, in the first place, the condemnation of Satan, the ruler of this world **(Colossians 2:15)**. However, the Holy Spirit will also convince the person in whom He creates faith of the certainty of the judgment that awaits all people. It is a judgment for sin and especially for the most heinous of sin—rejection of Jesus Christ.

5. In **16:12–13** Jesus promised His disciples that the Holy Spirit would open their understanding so that they would realize more fully the significance of what He said and did while He was among them as a human being.

6. The main message of the Holy Spirit is not about the future but about the past. The Spirit's function is not to satisfy our curiosity about what will happen but to open our understanding to what has happened in Jesus Christ. This complementary function of the Spirit is reemphasized in **16:14.** The special purpose of the Spirit is to bring glory to Jesus and to declare His mission and identity to the world.

7. This verse **(16:16)** refers primarily to the resurrection appearances of Jesus. However, it is also possible that Jesus was pointing to the disciples' seeing Him with the eyes of faith and the new appreciation that would be given them by the Holy Spirit after His ascension. Ultimately, Jesus will be seen again when "He is coming with the clouds, and every eye will see Him" **(Revelation 1:7).**

8. Just as the 11 disciples experienced sorrow **(16:20)** so there will come times in the life of every Christian when discipleship results in suffering of one sort or another and the sorrow that inevitably comes with it. But believers find comfort in the promise of Jesus that joy will follow sorrow.

9. Jesus urges us in **16:24** to ask God for what we wish. Because of Jesus we have a new relationship with God. We can call Him Father, and we can come to Him in the name of His Son. With this new relationship to God and the assurance that our prayers will be answered, our lives will be filled with joy.

10. In **16:27–28** Jesus claims to be the Son of God who has come from the Father and who is leaving this world to return to His Father. The disciples were having a hard time comprehending this, so Jesus repeated it once again.

The High Priestly Prayer (John 17)

1. We may be able to describe a person accurately and give much factual data about him and still say, "I don't really know him." To *know God* means much more than to be aware of certain facts about Him; it means understanding His precepts and will.

2. The gifts that the Father gave His Son were the people who believed in Him. **Ephesians 4:11** says that God still gives people as gifts to His church. The leaders of the Christian community are given to it by God. As **John 3:16** states, the greatest gift that God has given to our world is His Son, Jesus Christ.

3. Jesus was saying in **17:6** that by revealing God's name, He was revealing God Himself. It is apparent from the Old Testament passages cited that *God* can be substituted for *name* and the meaning is the same.

4. Jesus is certainly concerned about the world. He came to earth because of that concern. Indeed, here He was praying for His disciples specifically because He was leaving the earth, and His concern for the world would then have to be shown through them.

5. Here is a possible paraphrase for **17:11–12:** "Holy Father, protect them by the power that is You ... While I was with them, I protected them and kept them safe by the strength that is You."

6. The unity for which Jesus prayed is spiritual **(Ephesians 4:3–6);** a gift that gives great strength and joy to those who experience it. It is to be a powerful witness to the world that Jesus Christ, whom the church worships, is truly God's Son. We must ask ourselves to what extent the failure of the church to win the world for Jesus is due to outward disunity—not to mention exclusiveness, competition, and open hostility—among those who call themselves Christians. Furthermore, Christian unity is to show the world that God is, as they confess, a loving Father. Because He loves them they love one another and try to live at peace as His children.

7. Just as the sons of Aaron were consecrated—set apart—for priestly service in the temple **(Exodus 29)** so Jesus sets His followers apart for similar service. It is not in special buildings that their service is to be performed but in the entire world. As **Romans 12:1–2** states, the sacrifices we are to offer to God are not slaughtered animals but our own living bodies. The ordinary tasks of life, when consecrated to God, become the truest form of spiritual worship.

8. In **17:20–26** Jesus is praying for us. We are those who would come to faith long after He had returned to the Father. It should be particularly comforting to remember that we were the people on our Lord's mind and in His prayer on the night before His crucifixion. His prayer for us is

a. that we may live in unity with one another;

b. that we may live in unity with Him and the Father;

c. that we may live with Him in glory;

d. that we may live in the love of God, the same love the Father has for His Son.

The Word for Us

It might be best to choose one of these questions and spend some time discussing it.

1. If you choose to discuss this topic, try to keep the exchange positive. Talk about the ways in which Christians can express their unity. There are probably evidences of disunity in your own congregation. Talk about how the Gospel of forgiveness can be a healing force where there is disunity. Avoid blaming or faultfinding. Jesus' prayer for unity includes a prayer for the expression of spiritual unity. How can we avoid obscuring that unity?

2. This question is more personal. Many people suffer from a feeling of unimportance, a lack of personal purpose and value. It is not possible to improve their opinion of themselves by talking. But the knowledge that Jesus Himself holds them in great value and has a purpose for them can be the start of personal growth for them. Talk about some ways in which the message is meaningful for individuals in the class. Let them share their experiences with their feelings of worthlessness and how the Gospel has been important in their own struggle for personal worth and fulfillment.

Closing

Follow the suggestion in the Study Guide. Then close with prayer, asking the Holy Spirit to guide you and to keep you strong in faith so that you may be one with each other in the Lord.

Lesson 12

The End and ... (John 18–19)

Before the Session

If possible, read about the customs of Passover before reading through **John 18–19.** As always, check out the comfort level of the classroom ahead of time.

Getting Started

Open with a prayer thanking Jesus for His suffering and death, which bought your salvation. Pray for open hearts and minds for your study time. Then have volunteers read the "Theme Verse" and "Goal."

What's Going On Here

This is the climax of the Gospel—the crucifixion of Jesus. However you handle this material, be sure you help the class see that "God was reconciling the world to Himself in Christ" (**2 Corinthians 5:19**). Read through the paragraph under this section in the Study Guide to introduce the lesson.

Searching the Scriptures

Jesus' Arrest and the Appearance before the High Priest (John 18:1–27)

1. The word used in **18:3** for "a detachment of soldiers" is *speira*. It is a military term and usually refers to a cohort of 600 Roman soldiers, although sometimes it was used to describe a smaller detachment (usually known as a *maniple*) that numbered around 200 soldiers.

Far from running away, Jesus strode defiantly forward to meet His captors and then asked whom they were seeking. The response of Jesus (**18:5**) is literally "I am." (See the previous discussion in connection with **6:20** and **8:24**.) This phrase goes back to **Exodus 3:14,** where God identified Himself to Moses with these words.

2. The power of God resides in Jesus. By a word He can overwhelm His enemies. He made it clear that He could not have been taken captive if He had not willed it. Besides, as His comment to Peter in **Matthew 26:51–54** indicates, Jesus had resources at His disposal that no one else was aware of.

3. "The cup the Father has given Me" (**18:11**) is the suffering that was necessary for Jesus to endure in order to save the world. It was God's "gift," appointed by Him for Jesus. We are reminded of Jesus' prayer in the Garden of Gethsemane, which the synoptic gospels contain (**Matthew 26:36–46; Mark 14:32–42; Luke 22:39–46**) and which John may be alluding to here. John did not record the event of Jesus praying in the Garden.

4. The other disciple referred to in **18:15–16** cannot be identified with certainty. Some have thought he was a disciple whose name was unknown to John. Others have suggested Nicodemus or Joseph of Arimathea, who were both members of the Sanhedrin and so would be known to the high priest. The traditional view is that John is here referring to himself. That, however, poses a problem: How could a common fisherman from Galilee be known to the high priest?

5. In the Garden of Gethsemane Peter alone drew his sword in an attempt to defend Jesus against hopeless odds (**18:10**). He could see that

he had no real chance against the armed soldiers but he was ready to risk his life for Jesus, as he said he would **(13:37)**. Furthermore, except for the unnamed disciple Peter was the only one who followed Jesus into the courtyard of the high priest's house. If the others did not deny Jesus as Peter did, it was only because they did not show the courage that Peter did. He alone put himself in the position where he eventually was cornered.

Jesus before Pilate (John 18:28–19:16)

1. According to Jewish ceremonial law, the homes of Gentiles were unclean. In addition, the Passover was the Feast of Unleavened Bread. In preparation for it the Jews got rid of any leaven (yeast) that they had in their homes. Just entering a dwelling that contained leaven was considered to be contaminating. Therefore, the Jews would not enter Pilate's official residence on two counts. They were meticulous in the observance of their religious regulations, while at the same time plotting and executing the death of the innocent Son of God.

2. John did not recount the outcome of the interrogation by the high priest. Mark made it clear that the trial before the Sanhedrin ended with Jesus condemned for blasphemy **(Mark 14:61–64)**. From the question that Pilate asked Jesus in **18:33** it is apparent that the Jews had changed their charge. Before Pilate they masked the real cause of their hatred against Jesus by charging Him with being a revolutionary, a man who posed a threat to Caesar and the Roman rule of Palestine by claiming to be a king.

3. There are some questions you cannot answer with a simple yes or no. Pilate's question to Jesus whether He is a king is one of these. Jesus wanted to find out if this question came directly from Pilate (who may have wanted to determine if Jesus was a rebel) or if it originated with the Jews. Jesus' further responses would depend on whether Pilate was acting alone or as an ambassador for the Jews.

4. Pilate understood neither *kingship* nor *truth*. We cannot tell what he meant by his question, "What is truth?" Was he being sarcastic, ironic, wistful, or honestly inquisitive? Regardless of how we interpret his question, the answer was standing right in front of him. Jesus, whom he asked, is "the Truth." This was only one of the many ironies of the trial before Pilate.

5. Pilate could see that Jesus was no threat to the Roman government. He could see, too, the antagonism of the Jewish leaders. By flogging Jesus Pilate hoped to evoke pity from the crowd and satisfy the anger of the leaders.

6. In **19:7** the Jews state the real reason for their antagonism. It had

nothing to do with politics. They understood well enough the claim that Jesus had made. In our day there are those who maintain that Jesus never claimed to be divine. But there is only one thing that can explain the kind of hostility that was directed against Jesus—His claim to be the Son of God.

7. It was obvious to Jesus that there was no way Pilate would understand Him. There was no point in trying to communicate. Jesus was similarly silent before the high priest **(Mark 14:61)** and Herod **(Luke 23:9)**.

8. In **19:12** the Jews tried to blackmail Pilate. They pretended to be loyal subjects of Rome, aghast at the thought that a Roman governor would free a man who, they claimed, set Himself against the emperor. The implication of their remarks, understood by Pilate, was that, should he release Jesus, they would see that word of his action got back to Rome.

9. On the Day of Preparation the lambs for the Passover feast were slaughtered. It was while they were being killed that Jesus, the *Lamb of God*, was led out to be put to death.

10. In the prolog John said, "He came to that which was His own, but His own did not receive Him" **(1:11)**. When the Jews cried, "We have no king but Caesar" **(John 19:15)**, they were speaking the tragic truth. They had rejected God's Messiah-King.

Jesus' Crucifixion and Burial (John 19:17–42)

1. Pilate had his superscription written in the languages that would give his sarcasm the widest publicity.

2. As part of the Passover celebration the door of every Jewish house was sprinkled with hyssop dipped in the blood of the paschal lamb. This had been done on the night before the exodus from Egypt; all houses so marked were saved from the angel of death. Jesus is the Christian Paschal Lamb whose blood was shed to save all those who believe in Him.

3. When Jesus cried, "It is finished," He was saying much more than "It is over; I am about to die." This final word was not a weary sigh of resignation but a triumphant shout of victory: "It has been accomplished. The Father's plan of salvation is complete!"

4. The water and blood that flowed from Jesus' pierced side remind us of things He had said to describe Himself and of the sacraments He had given to the church.

The Word for Us

1. This question is designed to help participants get past the listing of events recorded in these chapters and onto the meaning of the events. There are two ways you can carry out this sharing session:

a. As a class, select a character and share openly in the class about that character. Encourage all the members to add something from their sense of the person and his/her experience. Concentrate on trying to make the person under discussion a real person with strengths and weaknesses. The purpose is to see how we, like that person, need the crucifixion for our salvation.

b. Assign characters to individual members of the class for research and later discussion. If this is done, set aside a time for this sharing at the next class meeting. Encourage the participants to develop a personal sketch of the person and to expose some of that character's strengths and weaknesses. The purpose, again, is to make the characters real and demonstrate their need, as well as ours, for the salvation of the cross.

2. The message of these chapters is Law and Gospel. Discuss how the knowledge that our sin put Jesus on the cross both exposes our sinfulness and condemns us. Then emphasize that the most important message of the cross is the message that the salvation bought there is for each of us as individuals. Let the class members share their favorite portions of these chapters. Encourage them to indicate what is meaningful about those words for them.

Closing

Follow the suggestion in the Study Guide. Then close with a prayer, confessing your sins that nailed Jesus to the cross, and praising Him for the forgiveness that He won there.

Lesson 13

... the Beginning (John 20–21)

Before the Session

Read through these chapters before class. What new insights did you gain from them? For this last session, don't forget to get to the classroom early to make sure it is set up correctly.

Getting Started

Begin with a prayer asking the risen Jesus to provide you understanding as you study His Word. Then have volunteers read the "Theme Verse" and "Goal."

What's Going On Here

These chapters are the culmination of the gospel of John. Here the miracles all come together in the resurrected Jesus. Here the crucifixion victory is proclaimed. Try to convey to the class both the excitement and wonder that must have been a part of the Easter experience recorded here. The paragraphs in the Study Guide under this heading point to that wonder—you may want to read them aloud. Or you might read aloud the touching personal encounters Jesus had with Mary **(20:11–18)**, Thomas **(20:26–29)**, and Peter **(21:15–19)**. Talk about how these people must have felt during and after their encounters with the risen Lord.

Searching the Scriptures

The Resurrection (John 20)

1. Peter was still the recognized leader of the disciples. It was to him that Mary went with the report of the empty tomb.

2. As **20:2** indicates, Mary Magdalene was no more expecting to find the tomb empty than were the disciples.

3. The fact that the burial clothes were found in the tomb and that they were neatly folded refutes the suggestion that the disciples, or anyone else, had stolen the body. No one doing that would have stripped the body of its wrappings, let alone taken the time to fold them carefully. John specifically wanted to note this one small verification of the resurrection.

4. In **20:9** John means that they did not understand the passages in the Old Testament which, under the guidance of the Holy Spirit, they later came to realize were spoken of the resurrection of Jesus. In **2:22** John says much the same thing in a slightly different way: "After He was raised from the dead, His disciples recalled what He had said. Then they believed the Scripture and the words that Jesus had spoken."

5. Mary mistook Jesus for the gardener for three simple reasons. First, she was certain Jesus was dead and that His body had been taken away. Second, her eyes were filled with tears. Third, Mary was looking in the wrong direction. When she turned **(20:16)** she could see and recognize Jesus.

6. From Jesus' response in **20:17,** we know that Mary must have grasped Jesus in some manner. In **Matthew 28:9** we read what the women did when they met Jesus: "They came to Him, *clasped His feet* and worshiped Him." Mary, apparently, had done the same thing that the women in Matthew's account did. She meant to say by her action, "Now that I have found You, I am never going to let You go." But Jesus had other plans. Though Mary found it hard to understand, what Jesus had said to the disci-

ples was true: "I tell you the truth: It is for your good that I am going away" (16:7).

7. Mary offers a good example of witnessing: She had contact with Jesus; she went to people she knew and told about her experience (20:18). That is what Christianity is—union with the living Lord. Witnessing is telling others about Jesus and about the way that union with Him makes a difference in your life.

8. In 20:21 Jesus puts His church in mission. *Mission* comes from the Latin word *mitto* which means "to send." The church is to be a going group. As God sent His Son into the world (3:17), so the Son sends His church, His body, to continue what He began. The Father had sent His Son to restore the unity that we had lost through sin. That is the mission on which we are sent by our Lord (17:18, 21–23; 11:52).

9. John wrote "with that He breathed on them" (20:22) to encourage his readers to think back to the Genesis account of creation. There God "*breathed* into his nostrils the *breath* of life, and the man became a living being" (Genesis 2:7, emphasis added). Jesus breathed life into His *new creation*, the church, in the same way that God breathed life into Adam.

10. In Mark's account of the healing of a paralyzed man, the scribes asked, "Who can forgive sins but God alone?" (Mark 2:7). While it is true that only God can forgive sin, it is the great commission of the church to proclaim and convey the message of God's forgiveness to the world.

11. Because Thomas had isolated himself from the rest of the disciples he missed Jesus. He was more alone than he realized. Thomas wanted not only to see but to touch and handle before he would believe. Was John perhaps referring to Thomas when he wrote 1 John 1:1?

12. Discuss whether it would be easier to believe if you were a disciple who lived with Jesus every day or to be a modern-day believer with the benefit of the written word.

13. John wrote that Jesus is "the Christ, the Son of God" (20:31). His hope was that all who read his account would come to the same conclusion and would experience the eternal life of God.

The Risen Lord Shows Himself (John 21)

1. Peter was an activist. He was often the spokesman for the Twelve (Mark 8:29; 9:5). He took the lead. So here (21:7) he impetuously hurled himself into the water in order to get to Jesus as quickly as possible. It was "the disciple whom Jesus loved," however, who was the first to realize the true identity of the man on shore. It was he whose testimony undergirds the entire gospel (21:24).

2. In the account of a similar catch of fish recorded in Luke 5:1–11

Peter's reaction was that he was unworthy, a "sinful man." After his triple denial of Jesus he had to be even more aware of his shortcomings.

3. Many intricate and ingenious interpretations of **21:11** have been given and can be found in any commentary. There are times when we must admit that we don't know exactly what is meant. This is one of those instances. The simplest approach is to take the story as it stands, without attaching symbolism to it. One old explanation is that the number 153 symbolizes perfection or wholeness and points to the time when men of all nations will be gathered together to Jesus Christ. Some take the unbroken net as representing the church, which can accommodate all people.

4. The threefold repetition of the question to Peter is perhaps an allusion to his threefold denial. If so, it was Jesus' way of allowing Peter to replace his triple denial with a triple affirmation of his love. The response of Jesus, "Feed My lambs. ... Take care of My sheep. ... Feed my sheep," was Peter's reinstatement to a position of leadership and of work. Jesus would still make use of him.

5. Jesus predicted the way Peter would die **(20:18)**. According to tradition, Peter was crucified in Rome; but he asked to be nailed to the cross head down because he said he was not worthy to die as his Lord had died. To die in obedience and faithful service to God is to glorify Him **(21:19)**. See also **13:31; 15:8; 17:1**.

The Word for Us

1. If you have not done so, use the three encounters indicated in "What's Going On Here" and in the Study Guide as a way of making the message of the Easter resurrection real for the members of your class.

a. Mary's grief was real **(20:11–18)**. Her lonely withdrawal and weeping were exactly what one would expect of a person who was grieving. Encourage the participants to share times of their own grief. The story gives the opportunity to connect the hope of the resurrection to the event of grief in your class members' lives.

b. Thomas doubted **(20:26–29)**. He struggled with the need that has afflicted people since the beginning of time: the need for proof. Let participants share times of doubt or despair. Use the positive action of Jesus toward Thomas, even in the midst of his doubt, as reassurance that doubt does not separate us from Christ. He continues to seek us, call us back, and forgive.

c. Peter suffered with guilt. Encourage class members to share their guilt—though it is not necessary for them to tell of specific sins. Remind them of the forgiveness that Christ through the church (the people of God) has to offer. Help them realize that Peter was not rejected but challenged after he was forgiven.

2. Discuss practical ways in which the joyful message of Easter can be shared. Be positive. Accept all suggestions, whether they be "evangelism programs," or simple, personal expressions of faith. Help the class to see that we witness as we live the joyful eternal life we have been given through the resurrection of Jesus Christ. Faith qualifies us as witnesses.

Closing

Follow the suggestion in the Study Guide. Then close with a prayer, praising our risen Savior for the wonderful deeds He has done.